AF248571

Atlanta in the Age of Pericles

ATLANTA IN THE AGE OF PERICLES

By

James Sage Jenkins

CHIMNEY HILL PRESS
4303 Highway 124
Lithonia, Georgia 30058

Books by James Sage Jenkins

MURDERS AND SOCIAL CHANGE
MURDER IN ATLANTA

Books by Herbert T. Jenkins in association with
James Sage Jenkins

KEEPING THE PEACE
FORTY YEARS ON THE FORCE
ATLANTA AND THE AUTOMOBILE
ATLANTA FAIRS AND FARMERS' MARKETS
PRESIDENTS POLITICS AND POLICING
CRIME IN GEORGIA

LIMITED FIRST EDITION

Darby Printing Company
Atlanta, Georgia

Library of Congress Catalogue Number: 79-55432
International Standard Book Number: 0-89937-029-2

ACKNOWLEDGEMENTS

A very special acknowledgement to Margaret and Witt Gordon McAndrew without whose support and assistance this book would never have been published.

I would also like to give credit to three individuals who contributed greatly to this book who did not live to see it published: My mother, who provided much of the information on the James Wideman Lee family; my great uncle, Miles Herbert Mason, Senior, who witnessed and recounted to me Margaret Mitchell's visits to Gwinnett County, Georgia; and, to my aunt, Erna Lee Mason, for providing invaluable research and advice.

And lastly, to my good friend, Loris Hamilton, of New York City, whose incisive editing allowed me to bring this remembrance of a time in the history of the city of Atlanta more clearly into focus.

In Memory of
Carolyn R. Reynolds
and
D. Patrick Coleman

Contents

Atlanta in the Age of Pericles

ONE

THENCEFORWARD AND FOREVER FREE

The power of vested interest is vastly exaggerated compared with the gradual encroachment of ideas.
John Maynard Keynes, *The General Theory*

We sat there silently in the rear of the council chamber of Atlanta's city hall. The large assembly area had been converted into a giant press room for the national and foreign press corps. We stared at a television screen waiting for President Kennedy's new conference from Washington to begin. It seemed like we had been waiting for an awfully long time.

The day had begun very early for all of us, on this Monday, this August 30th, 1961. It was an historic day for Atlanta and Georgia and America. Without incident ten black high school students had been enrolled at four previously all white schools. The Atlanta wall of Segregation, though not shattered, had been breached, and the Southern way of life that had been practiced in Atlanta was well on its way to becoming history.

The room grew silent. The press conference was about to begin. Then all at once, President Kennedy was on television. Before beginning his previously scheduled press conference he began reading a prepared statement.

"I want to take this opportunity to congratulate Mayor Hartsfield of Atlanta, Chief of Police Jenkins . . ."

As the President began speaking, Helen Bullard, who was sitting next to me, sort of bent forward, not so much to better hear the President, for a hushed silence pervaded the room, but to be sure what she was seeing and hearing was not a dream.

> ". . . and all of the parents, students and citizens of Atlanta, Georgia, for the responsible, law abiding manner in which four high schools were Desegregated today . . ."

Helen managed to stifle crying-out by placing her right hand over her mouth and simultaneously reached toward me with her left hand just as I was reaching toward her and we clasped each others' hand tightly and held onto one another as President Kennedy continued.

> ". . . this was the result of vigorous efforts for months by the officials of Atlanta and by groups of citizens throughout the community . . ."

For all of us who had worked so long to end Segregation in the South, John F. Kennedy, thirty-fifth President of the United States, was our champion. Only when *he* confirmed that the events in Atlanta that day had actually happened did we believe it to be true.

> ". . . their efforts have borne fruit in the orderly manner in which the Desegregation was carried out . . . with dignity and without incident. Too often in the past such steps have been marred by violence and disrespect for law . . ."

President Kennedy was neither the first nor last president to publicly thank my father for his efforts to bring an end to Segregation in the South, but his words were the most significant because his support came at the critical time of the struggle.

> ". . . I strongly urge the officials and citizens of all communities which face this difficult transition in the coming weeks and months to look closely at what Atlanta has done . . . and to meet their responsibility, as the officials of Atlanta have done, with courage, tolerance, and above all, respect for the law."

When the President had concluded his statement on Atlanta Helen and I leaped to our feet and embraced each other in a victorious bear hug. It was as though we had just climbed Mt. Everest. That is the way we both felt. It was a very private and emotional moment for us. We were totally oblivious to our surroundings, or the people in the crowded chamber. We were alone on our own mountain top.

Eventually, Helen and I came down from our high and realized that people were fast emptying the chamber. Mayor Hartsfield, who had so carefully orchestrated the events of the day, came by on his way out. With very few words to mark the momentous occasion, he attempted to be all business and presented himself to us as the busy mayor of Atlanta who was merely winding-up another hard day at the office. Right away, he said to Helen that they had work to do and the two of them moved toward the mayor's office. I stayed on until everyone else had left the council chamber.

Atlanta was certainly an interesting place to be living as the last days of Segregation began fading into the Southern twilight. In this remarkable time the legal foundation supporting the South's Segregationist laws began developing cracks. Ultimately it would collapse altogether, and when the debris of the past was swept away a new way of living would replace the old structure so long the dominant force gracing the Dixie landscape.

The future would see the South transformed into the Eastern anchor of the Sun-belt.

The people and places and policies in the South which made this possible, in circumstances nowadays occurring all over the globe, provide a partial enlightenment to some of the more pressing problems of our time. If indeed, we view history as prologue, certainly in this instance the *Second Battle of Atlanta* occurring in the mid-twentieth century is instructive toward ways of living in the new century looming upon our horizon.

In the era of Segregation, Daylight Saving Time had yet to be implemented and by the time I left city hall it was dusk. Helen had urged all the businesses in the downtown office buildings to keep all their lights burning late into the night as a positive beacon commemorating the historic events of the day; and most had complied.

I walked alone through the city's streets, marveling that people were going about their business in the usual manner. But of course, that was the point: The beginning of a huge social transformation had occurred peacefully and no violence had marred the day, and this meant that the people of the South could get

on with their lives—and anything was possible. The shackles
which had made Black people second-class citizens, had impris-
oned the hearts and minds of white people in prejudice, and had
kept the South the backward colony of the rest of America, had,
at long last, been removed.

In the late August evening of 1961 the words President Kennedy spoke kept pounding in my brain as I continued walking
the streets of the city.

> "I strongly urge the officials and citizens of all communities
> which face this difficult transition in the coming weeks and
> months to look closely at what Altanta and Georgia have done,
> with courage, tolerance . . ."

I had no idea whether the people of the South would heed
President Kennedy's advice, and, in fact, gave it little thought.
My mind that night was filled not with the great promise of Atlanta's and the South's future, but the events of the past which
had so dominated my life; for, at age twenty-five, I was the same
age as the number of years it took for the final and conclusive
battle to end Segregation to be won.

Exactly ten years before he became president, John F. Kennedy, was aware of Atlanta's effort to lead the South away from
the cobwebs of its history. He let Atlanta leaders know then, and
many times again during the intervening years, that he was on
their side and that they could count on him as an ally.

It was therefore impossible to imagine that what had occurred
in Atlanta could have happened without him. The two were totally linked in my thinking that evening and it was impossible
for me to imagine Desegregation occurring in Atlanta with anyone other than Kennedy as president.

As I gazed upward at the lights illuminating the Atlanta sky-
line, I was just so very thankful that President Kennedy had
supported Atlanta's leaders and had made this such a glorious
day for the people of Atlanta and with his statement had given
such a meaningful and eloquent conclusion to all our endeavors.

TWO

TERMINUS

Pre-Civil War Atlanta was a dirty, smoke-filled, frontier kind of place. The air was filled with soot and cinders from the wood-burning steam engines that brought trains in and out of town all day long.

Atlanta came into existence in the early 1840s because it was the spot in Georgia where the Western and Atlantic Railroad halted. It stopped in the middle of nowhere because state funds for railroad building had been exhausted and established Georgia cities feared that the introduction of the steam engine into their tranquil towns would encroach upon their way of living. It is an anomaly, but the largest city in Georgia is also one of the youngest.

Passengers and freight from the north and west enroute to the Atlantic coast port of Savannah, had to take a stage coach from the point where the rails of the Western and Atlantic ended, farther south, to where the railroad was finished. The building of railroads in the 19th century followed a pattern similar to construction of interstate highways in the 20th century. There were gaps and endless repairs and re-routings which for a multitude of reasons, took forever to complete.

Irish immigrants had landed at the port of Savannah in the 1800s lured there by the promise of jobs in building railroads westward. The stalwart Irish first brought the rails across the sandy swampland of mosquito infested South Georgia—and finally connected with the Western and Atlantic Railroad at what came to be called Atlanta.

The new place was called Atlanta because it was the terminal point of the Western and Atlantic Railroad southward, and the name Atlanta was a made up designation from Atlantic. Railroad personnel wrote *Atlanta* on baggage and passenger tickets of those traveling to the terminus of the Western and Atlantic Railroad.

In later years, to enhance the city's image, eager Atlanta Promoters (though not all that well-versed in Greek mythology) would promulgate the legend which still persists that Atlanta was the namesake of Atalanta, the goddess of fleetness and strength.

W.E.B. DuBois, a resident of Atlanta during the time when the Atalanta myth was taking hold, stated if the city had not it certainly should have been named for Atalanta because when in a race against her suitors in which the penalty for losing was loss of life, Atalanta lost both the race and her life because she was lured into stopping during the contest to pick up three golden apples.

In bringing the railroad westward, the Irish workers kept collecting excess baggage as they moved along. An assortment of individuals of Native American, African, and European descent followed the tracks to Atlanta. There was nothing there except the excitement people feel when involved in something new.

At the juncture of the railroads this polygot of people landed and camped out. Soon the settlement started moving away from the railroad tracks, but the site never had a basic plan of development or was properly laid out. There was no town square or planned parallel streets running north and south or east and west. Atlanta streets were as crooked as cowpaths, indeed many followed livestock trails, and every person built on his property to suit himself. Very few people believed there would ever be much of a town in this location because there was nothing to attract people but the railroad terminus.

People in the place worked on the railroads. When they were not working on the railroads they drank and fought with each other and over the few unmarried women in town. Atlanta was a tough place to live and had all the riotous behavior common not only to frontier towns but railroad towns as well. There was no sense of city or tradition.

One of the Irish foremen working on the railroad wanted to bring his wife to Atlanta. When the lady learned that Atlanta cabins were not floored she refused to move to the new place and join her husband unless her cabin was floored with planks. The foreman's wife should not be expected to live in a shack with a dirt floor and not until her husband installed a wooden floor in their cabin did she join him in Atlanta.

No sooner was she settled in than she decided to hold a dance on her new floor and invited all the workers and their wives. This first recorded social function held in Atlanta was such a success that all the other wives demanded that wooden floors be installed in their cabins in order that they could entertain socially. Thus from such humble beginnings began Atlanta's future well-deserved reputation as a very friendly, socially-minded party town.

The more affluent planters who resided upon plantations in the near-by countryside, and regarded themselves as English gentry, were scandalized. Atlanta was one of those wickedly Biblical places to be shunned. They were grateful that the railroad had not come their way.

This very same geographic area comprising Atlanta and the adjacent countryside which today is most often referred to as Greater Atlanta, is inhabited by people who reside in Atlanta and those who live in newer, well-planned suburban communities. Many of those now residing in the countryside of the 19th century maintain the same view of the central city as the residents of those times and never venture into downtown Atlanta. Many who are recent new-comers to Greater Atlanta have never even visited the downtown area, for like their 19th century counterparts, they live their lives sufficient unto themselves, and whereas today shopping centers and malls have replaced farms and plantations as the source of all bounty, the citizens of Atlanta carry on the early tradition of trying to make the city a better place in which to live.

During this early time when Atlanta was still in its embryo days of development, a number of famous personages of the time passed through town on their way somewhere else. One such visitor was John C. Calhoun of South Carolina. Calhoun observed since Atlanta was the terminus point for railroad travel westward it would grow into a major transportation center as the steam engine replaced the stagecoach as the primary means of travel as American expanded westward. Calhoun, who was wrong about everything else, was right about Atlanta.

Another visitor passing through town in this era was a young, red-headed, U.S. Army lieutenant who spent six weeks along the Western and Atlantic railroad and the surrounding countryside on assignment for the Army. During his visit the lieutenant familiarized himself with the land from Atlanta north to Tennessee. This Army task gave the young West Point graduate the opportunity to observe at close range the terrain of northeast Georgia.

The young lieutenant passed through Atlanta with little notice. But when he returned some two decades later as head of the Union Army of the Tennessee, the passing of General William Tecumseh Sherman through Atlanta on his march to the sea was a journey not unknown to any resident of the state of Georgia.

THREE

THE RED EARTH

Until the coming of the railroads, towns which grew into important cities were located on rivers and/or seaports. The act of the Georgia legislature creating the Western and Atlantic railroad mandated the southwestern tracks of the railroad cross the Chattahoochee River and proceed to a point not to exceed eight miles from the river. At this spot the railroad ended and Atlanta came into existence independent of any waterway. Henceforth the only need railroads would have for water as an aid to transportation would be in creating steam to propel the train engines.

The site where the Atlanta zero mile post was hammered into the red soil (the earth is red because it contains an abundance of granite laced with iron and when exposed to rain oxidation occurs and "bleeds" the soil red) was on a high ridge in the foothills of the Blue Ridge Mountains 1,050 feet above sea level. Such a height provided Atlanta with a Summer climate less humid than other Southern cities. It was also a healthier climate and Atlanta was not prone to malaria or other 19th century epidemics. The watershed on which Atlanta is located drains into both the Atlantic Ocean and the Gulf of Mexico. It is said that the rainwater which falls upon Atlanta's most famous thoroughfare, Peachtree Street, on one side drains into the Atlantic and on the other into the Gulf. The elevation and natural drainage system renders Atlanta free of floods. It also made it possible in the latter half of the 20th century to erect office towers in Atlanta without the added cost of re-building the city's drainage system.

In the census of 1850 the new cities that had attained 2,000 or more population appeared for the first time. Among these were San Francisco, St. Paul, San Antonio, Los Angeles and—

Atlanta.

It was as though nature had provided the place to connect the South with the rest of the country, for with the completion of the railroads to other Southern cities Atlanta became the crossroads of trade and commerce. This made the city a cotton marketing hub. Because it was a cotton marketing center it became a cotton manufacturing center. Other commodities were important in the South but cotton dominated everything else. Cotton and the railroads made Atlanta an important place: It was on the cuting edge of the new technology.

Then, as now, as a consequence, the promise of quick fortunes to be made provided the impetus for people to flock to Atlanta.

Decatur Street was the main east-west artery and intersected with Peachtree Street at the center of town. Decatur Street has always been Atlanta's colorful crossroads crowded with both white and African-American small business proprietors, newly arrived foreigners speaking languages no one understood, and drifters on the make. In its heyday there was no other place in the South quite like it because it had an aura of Eastern Europe and the middle East enveloping its inhabitants.

In the earliest days Decatur Street had been the sight of the first sawmill in Atlanta. It was the first business to operate in Atlanta and people rode in from miles around to look at it. The sawmill was something new and its power was supplied by a blind mule which became a source of much interest for everybody. The rumor spread the owner fed his mule only sawdust and this absurdity became part of the folklore. The mill supplied lumber for building railroads, and it was a lucrative business since trees could be had just for the cutting, and the land was covered in virgin forest which needed clearing to provide building lots for the growing population. As Atlanta prospered the sawmill moved farther out and the grounds became the sight of the first Atlanta city jail.

The jail was a one-room cabin and it was called the lockup. The lock for the door was made of wood but the metal key was almost a foot long and very heavy. It impressed those who were arrested—mostly drunks—until they sobered up the next day.

Law enforcement was the responsibility of a sole town marshal and he had his hands full in keeping order. For every fifty people in the town there was a saloon. There was also an extremely large number of restless youths who roamed the city harassing law-abiding citizens.

One day the town marshal was sitting on his horse with a crowd of youngsters in front of him. He was lecturing to them and telling them they should mend their ways when one youth slipped up behind the marshal's horse and tied a string of firecracks to the horse's tail. When the firecrackers began exploding the horse bucked and threw the marshal off onto the muddy street and ran away. Very shortly, the first schoolhouse was built in Atlanta.

During the Civil War Atlanta was invaded, defeated, occupied by Northern troops, and then burned. With the arrival of General Sherman in Atlanta in 1864, the city went under U.S. Military rule. Following the departure of Sherman and the burning of Atlanta, the governor of Georgia sent in the state militia to help restore order. Later, during the era of Reconstruction, U.S. military rule was once again imposed by the Federal government.

The assault on the civilian population of Atlanta during the seige of the city by General Sherman during the Civil War is known to millions of people worldwide from *Gone With The Wind*. Cities everywhere to this very day have suffered such assaults since time immemorial. But it was unique for an American city to undergo such a wartime experience. The chaotic evacuation of the Army defending Atlanta so graphically portrayed in the "Burning of Atlanta" sequence of *Gone With The Wind* can only be comprehended by Americans of today when compared with the defeat and withdrawal in the 1970s of the American Army from Saigon. It was a new experience for Americans to suffer such a humiliating military defeat and it strongly affected Vietnam veterans and their fellow countrymen and all future generations of Americans. Those who fought and lost and survived the Battle of Atlanta were similarly affected not only in the time of the civil War but for generations to follow—all the way to the present day. In both wars the losers had to lick their wounds and ponder the rightness and wrongness of their actions and suffer the guilt of not only losing but wondering if they were even fighting for the proper cause.

By 1869 the last Federal troops had withdrawn from Atlanta. The city was once again on its own. The railroads, which had been destroyed in the war, were rebuilt.

From the point where the railroads met, the city began to build outward once again. Ten years later Sherman returned to Atlanta on a goodwill visit and could not believe his eyes. He was met at the train station by a large and friendly crowd who were anxious to show the man who had burned down most of Atlanta how well they had done in rebuilding.

Although the rebuilding of Atlanta would have been an excellent opportunity to indulge in some extensive city planning this did not happen. There was not enough time. Rebuilding after the war was a rush project because people wanted to start making money again. Members of the old planter class which had been so snooty about the railroad and Atlanta in the past, now began moving to town to start businesses.

As Atlanta was busy rebuilding its physical structure much of the rest of the South was busily reshaping its social system.

A form of slavery existed in the South well into the 20th century. It was called Segregation. If the people of the South could not have a separate nation then they were determined to have a separate economic, political, and social set-up.

When the United States Supreme Court struck down the last of the Reconstruction laws passed by Congress during the Civil War period, and in 1869 ruled in Plessy versus Ferguson that laws segregating people because of their race did not violate the United States Constitution, the races in the South became totally separate.

By the opening of the new century, the South had not undergone a reconstruction but a restoration. Years had passed, the conomic system had been wrecked, but the social ways were as true in 1900 as they had been in 1800. A system of rigid apartheid was enforced throughout the South and kept the colored individual in his or her place. Although many whites at first had resisted the restoration, they soon grasped the overwhelming sweep of the movement into Southern life.

Segregation affected all aspects of Southern life. An African-American could enter the home of white people only through the back door. On crowded city sidewalks, African-Americans were required to step off the curb and into the street to allow a white person to pass. All African-Americans were required to address white people as Mister or Mrs. or Miss.

Railroad passenger trains (air travel was very limited prior to World War II) had separate cars for blacks and whites. Trains from the North had to segregate the races before entering Dixie. The effect on black railroad passengers going South was that of entering a hostile foreign country.

Southern cities providing public transportation required black persons to board trolley cars from the rear and sit in the "back of the bus." Blacks were required to relinquish their seats to whites.

Tall buildings had "White Only" signs in the elevators. Blacks had to use freight elevators or climb the stairs. All eating establishments were rigidly segregated as were all colleges, private schools, public schools, libraries, hospitals, churches, movie theaters, baseball parks, golf courses, swimming pools, auditoriums, water fountains, dice games, checker games, dances, and waiting rooms.

Atlanta, like the rest of the South, converted to a segregated society. There was so much going on in Atlanta that the demagogues arrived along with the rest of the good folks on the make. But there was a difference. For a strict social code to be re-enforced it had to be pretty well defined in the first place. That had not been the case in Atlanta. Blacks could not be kept economically in an inferior status as easily as they could in the agricultural and the older, more traditional Southern places.

But as the rigid system of Segregation engulfed the South in a vise-like embrace, Atlanta, the most un-Southern of Southern places, was swiftly swept along.

Many people mistakenly believe that Atlanta has always been the capital of Georgia, when, in fact, during the ante bellum period no less than three other Georgia cities were the state capital. Only after the Civil War was the state capital moved to Atlanta. It was more easily accessible than anywhere else in Georgia because of the railroads. Being the capital city of the largest state east of the Mississippi River put the city in the center of things. In the center of Segregation.

As the Georgia legislature, along with all other Southern state legislatures began passing Segregation laws, Atlanta felt the impact. The city became as Segregated as the rest of the South. Although it had the most advanced black population in the state, it also headquartered the forces of legal Segregation in the state legislature and ultimately the terrorist arm of the political structure—the Ku Klux Klan. It was natural that Klan headquarters would follow the movement of the state legislature to Atlanta. It was the seat of power.

The South made Segregation effective by law and by custom and by intimidation. Any white person who did not support Segregation completely with both words and action was ostracized, insulted in various ways, and punished economically.

All fascists love fire in the night. The Klan was no different. On Saturday night members of the Ku Klux Klan, robed in their full regalia and their faces hooded, would gather at the highest point in every Southern town and city and ignite a huge flaming cross for all to see.

Everybody in the South in that time knew that the fire in the night meant that all governors, mayors, judges, and police officers were either Klan members or got their jobs and promotions with the support of the Ku Klux Klan.

Segregation dominated the Southern United States. Its enforcement arm, the Ku Klux Klan, existed for the same purposes and operated in the same manner, as the Gestapo did in Nazi Germany. This was not the situation in other places in the English speaking world. Segregation is what made the South different politically.

Stone Mountain. That monolith of giant-gray-granite sixteen miles from Atlanta, which centuries before had been the site of Native American religious ceremonies, became the Saturday night initiation spot for new Klan members. Amid flaming crosses which could be viewed by Atlanta residents, Klan strength grew and multiplied. Atlanta politicans and law officers were Klan members. The city's professional people were either Klan members or supported its aims. Everybody was not important enough to be a Klan member but nobody of any importance challenged the Klan ideology. It terrorized Blacks and frightened the ordinary white Southerner. It burned out any hope for dialogue or dissent.

In the Southern United States the KKK was referred to as the "Invisible Empire." It was called that because robed Klan members did not occupy political offices clad in their identifying garb. In ordinary situations they dressed like everybody else so as not to stand out. Only for parades and other public occasions did the Klan dress in their identifying uniforms.

Those in the South who opposed what the Klan stood for were called white Southern liberals by the Northern press. A kinder and gentler term for those who had made it impossible for Klan-thinkers to totally polarize the South. Throughout the Klan era Southern white liberals labored tirelessly to uplift the South, to educate its people, to end a way of living based upon fear.

Atlanta in the 1880s was a city of three capitals: Of the state of Georgia, of the "Invisible Empire," and of white Southern liberalism. No other place in the South could even come close to having the number of white forward-thinking liberals as were concentrated in Atlanta.

FOUR

IN THE LAND OF THE CHEROKEE ROSE

The first European to pass through the Greater Atlanta area was the Spanish conquistador, Hernando De Soto. After service under Pizarro in which he vigorously aided in the pillaging of Peru, he came through Georgia via Florida in 1540 on an expedition seeking gold and silver and jewels. He found no riches but he did "discover" the Cherokee Indians whom he robbed, enslaved, and murdered at will.

Two centuries, for which the Cherokees were everlastingly grateful, passed before other Europeans would arrive in the Atlanta area. When gold was discovered in the foothills of the Cherokee lands, the Cherokee nation was overrun with large numbers of New-world Europeans.

The Cherokee Indians inhabited the mountain areas of North and South Carolina, Georgia, Alabama, and Tennessee. It was the largest and most advanced single tribe in the southeastern United States. The men of the tribe hunted deer and other small game. The women raised corn, squash, and beans. Women held a high place in Cherokee society.

Much of the progress of the Cherokees was due to the invention of an alphabet by Sequoyah the son of a Cherokee woman and white trader. The 85 characters in the alphabet represented all the sounds in the Cherokee language and permitted the keeping of tribal records and, later, the translation of the Bible and other works into the Cherokee language.

Because they had a written language, more is known of Cherokee culture than of other, less advanced, American Indian tribes.

At the height of their power in the mid-eighteenth century, the Cherokee people suffered a severe smallpox epidemic brought on by their friendly association with the European new-comers, and as a result almost half the population perished.

Afterwards, the population stabilized at approximately 20,000 persons and by the 1820s the Cherokees had created a political system modeled upon the United States Constitution. The Cherokee capital, New Echota, located 65 miles northwest of Atlanta, was the Washington, D.C. of the Cherokee nation. There were fifty buildings in New Echota and the first Indian and first Georgia newspaper was printed there. For many years New Echota lay in ruins but was saved from destruction in the 1950s by local conservationists. It is now the site of a restored town of New Echota and state park.

By the early years of the 19th century the Cherokee Nation had sold or ceded much of the southeastern part of their territory to the United States government. In what might be termed 19th century leverged by-outs the Cherokee Indian country began to shrink as more and more of its acreage was acquired by land agents dedicated to moving the boundaries of the United States farther and farther westward.

Much of the land which Atlanta's present-day suburban sky-scrapers and shopping centers occupy was originally a segment of a larger portion of land in the area and was purchased by the United States government from the Cherokee Nation for $5,000 in cash and goods and a promised yearly payment of $1,000 making the Cherokees the first known purchasers of junk bonds.

Every time the United States moved westward the integrity of the Cherokee Nation was guaranteed by treaty. An honest effort was made to keep settlers off Indian land.

On May 20, 1820, a representative of the administration of President James Monroe, a soldier with vast experience in these matters, posted the following notice in what would become the Greater Atlanta area.

> Intruders on the Cherokee land beware. I am requested to remove all white men found trespassing on the Cherokee land not having permission . . . All white men with their stock found trespassing on Indian land will be arrested and handed over to the civil authority of the United States to be dealt with as the law directs, their families removed to the United States land, their crops, houses, and fences destroyed . . . This is to notify all such that are clearing and cultivating lands within the Indian boundary . . . that such improvements will be de-

stroyed and all persons found trespassing in this way will be seized and handed over to the marshal to be prosecuted . . .
To avoid trouble and expense this notice is given.

(signed) Andrew Jackson

The persons who could legally be on Cherokee land were those traders who had been given permission by Indian agents in accord with the Cherokees. If a white man married an Indian woman then the couple could legally reside in the Cherokee Nation. Since the entire state of Georgia was being rapidly populated by single white men who hoped to attain their own chunk of turf in the New World, inter-marriage among Cherokee women and Americans was occurring—more so than among any other American Indian tribe and European settlers. Orthodox Cherokee women viewed these mixed marriages with trepidation fearing they would be looked down upon in comparison because Cherokee women married to white men immediately adopted American ways of living and dress.

Thus, *all* Cherokee women began to dress almost universally in European-style clothing in dresses they made themselves from cotton they raised on their own plantations. Their daughters having grown up wearing European-styled clothing associated with, and married Americans, as a matter of course.

In spite of the best efforts of Andrew Jackson and the United States government, squatters could not be kept off Cherokee lands. There were so many land-hungry settlers pouring into the area it became an impossible task to separate the illegals from the legals. The Cherokees resented the squatters and the situation became tense. The Cherokees were an idealistic and cultured people but their tolerance of the squatters was being strained to the limit.

Along with the traders and white men married to Indian women, there were missionaries residing in the Indian territory. The atmosphere within the Cherokee Nation among Indians and Americans was friendly and the missionaries were attempting to improve the circumstances of the Cherokee people.

Many Georgians were upset by the seemingly permanence of the Cherokee Nation, and abhored the presence there of missionaries, who they regarded as established legal residents of a foreign power. If Cherokees became Christians it would be ever so much more difficult to get rid of them. For those individuals who thought like this, and they were in the majority, the problem was that the relationship among the citizens of the state of Georgia and the Cherokees, save for the problem of squatters, was one of two sovereign peoples who shared a common border, many similar social and economic concerns, and had a mutual respect for one another. This was a situation which expansionist-minded Georgians just could not abide.

The state of Georgia did not recognize the Indian territory as a nation, and argued that the United States Constitution prohibited an independent state from being formed inside a state's territory. Georgia made this argument before the U.S. Supreme Court and lost.

President Andrew Jackson, formally the defender of Indian rights did not like the decision, and declared, in his often quoted statement:

"Now that Chief Justice John Marhsall has made his decision, let him enforce it."

President Jackson insisted that the Cherokees had practically an "individual nation" inside Georgia and Alabama and he hoped that they would move west of the Mississippi River.

The state of Georgia enacted a Gold Lottery and began dispossessing Cherokees of their land in the area where gold had been discovered. The Cherokees were not equipped to deal with the gold rush, and appealed to the Federal government for protection. When their pleas fell on deaf ears the Cherokees were forced to move farther to the north and west.

A treaty was extracted from a small number of the Cherokee Nation which bound the entire tribe to remove west of the Mississippi River within three years. Although the whole tribe overwhelmingly repudiated this treaty, the die was cast.

The treaty called for the establishment of an Indian reservation in the Oklahoma territory. When the Cherokees refused to go they were removed by force and marched in mid-Winter to Oklahoma. Thousands died from being uprooted from their homes, along the march, and from the subsequent hardships. President Andrew Jackson refused to intervene although countless numbers of Cherokees and Americans urged him to do so. The removal of the Native Americans and the saga of their arduous journey is known as *The Trail of Tears*.

By the last decade of the twentieth century the northern suburbs of Atlanta had virtually overrun the Gold Lottery territory that had set in motion the series of events which led to the Trail of Tears.

Although the Cherokee were the most advanced Native Americans in Georgia they were by no means alone. Some fifty tribes lived along rivers and streams in Southern Georgia, Northern Florida, and Alabama. Although they were of the same linguistic stock, they were a diverse group. The European settlers lumped them all together and referred to them as the Creek Indians. The Creeks were generally agricultural, tall in height, had proud bearing, and loved ornamentation. They were less advanced than their northern neighbors. Whereas some of the Creek tribes were peaceful and congenial others were hostile and warlike. The fiercest of the war tribes were the Red Poles. They were aggressive and obsessed with fighting and war ceremonies. The entire Red Pole tribe was an army unit and resisted all encroachments from the north. When De Soto came through their neighborhood on his murderous march through the Indian lands, the Red Poles struck first. They surrounded the invaders, attacked and killed Spaniards and their guides, and seriously wounded De Soto.

Creek tribes waged war against the United States government and massacred not only whites but blacks and other Indians who did not support their warlike ways.

Andrew Jackson won his reputation as a soldier as a fighter at the battle of Horseshoe Bend, Alabama, which polished off the Creek War. Leading a force composed of Tennessee militiamen, Creek Indians loyal to the United States, and 600 Cherokees, he defeated 900 Red Pole warriors in a bloody encounter. The brilliant victory brought Andrew Jackson wide recognition and opened the way for his triumph in the Battle of New Orleans that made him a national hero and ultimately president of the United States. The remaining Creek tribes, like their Cherokee brethren were eventually removed to the Indian reservations in Oklahoma.

American history nowadays emphasizes the subjugation of Indians by Americans. Less emphasis is placed on the oppression of Indians by Indians and of other cultures. The Cherokees practiced slavery on their cotton plantations and African-Americans marched alongside their owners along the Trail of Tears. That great Indian Colossus of the North, the Iroquois, battled with other Indian tribes to expand its territory. The Iroquois waged war against the Cherokees in an endeavor to expand southward. Although their initial forays were checked, over time the Iroquois managed to annex some Cherokee land. In turn, the Cherokees pushed their nation farther south and conquered land once the exclusive domain of the Creek Indians.

It is also ironic that those Europeans wanting passionately to be free of the wars of the old world, came to America and immediately began waging war against the long established inhabitants who all along had been sticking it to their fellow compatriots.

The land upon which the city of Atlanta was built was Creek Indian territory. In continuous warfare the area became a battlefield of the Creeks against the Cherokee. The land was the Golan Heights between these two peoples who were constantly at war with one another.

Due east of Atlanta in an area including Stone Mountain and beyond, running along a continuous high ridge was the main trail, the north-south travel route, between the rival Indian tribes. For the Creeks, it was the gateway into the vast Cherokee Nation. For the Cherokee, it was a vital military passageway they fought to keep under their control. A process made easier if they kept the Creek Indians out of the immediate vicinity and away from Stone Mountain and the half-dozen other smaller monoliths located along the Indian trail.

For the Creeks, all the granite mountains in the area were sacred places. They held an annual green corn dance at the foot of Stone Mountain and at other stone outcroppings on their lands. The festival was a time for renewing social ties and a period of amnesty for prisoners. Old pots were broken, new fires lit. Then, dressed in new clothing, religious ceremonies were performed.

For their part, the Cherokee regarded the granite mountains as military outposts where their rivals could be observed, and if necessary, more easily attacked. Thus the area became the frontier between nations and sometimes a place for festivals; and other times of strategic military scouting. In between times, and since neither side could permanently settle in the vicinity, both sides used the land for growing crops. At various seasons, Creek and Cherokee women planted beans and squash. Insofar as the territory was not permanently settled by a dominant group, arriving English-speaking settlers referred to this frontier as the Indian Fields. The name endured even though festivals and military skirmishes continued at varied intervals. When the Indian Fields became a part of the United States and the Indians departed, the territory became a part of Gwinnett County, Georgia, and was quickly settled.

The county was named for Button Gwinnett one of three Georgians to sign the Declaration of Independence, who died shortly thereafter from injury suffered in a duel. Gwinnett was among the most obscure of the Founding Fathers. He had no male heirs and the family name passed from existence.

The newcomers of Gwinnett county planted cotton on the carefully cultivated terraces of the Cherokee and removed the rocks from the Creek Indian Mounds to build chimneys, line wells for drinking water, and serve as foundations for barns and houses. No one recorded what the departing Creek Indians had to say regarding these events.

The sacred relics of one culture become the building blocks of succeeding civilizations. South American settlements are dominated by imposing edifices built to honor the Christian God but occupying ground once dedicated to the worship of Native American gods. Succeeding generations of Egyptians stripped the polished granite facade of the great Pyramid to build a mosque in Cairo.

In no time at all, the Indian Fields turned white with cotton blooming in the furrows of prosperous plantation owners. Conditions for growing cotton in the Indian Fields were ideal and demand for Southern cotton was worldwide. The plantation owners grew prosperous.

The promise of equality had been the foundation upon which America was based, the reason for its existence. But because of its sudden wealth, the people in the South re-instituted the old European class system that in many instances they had fled to America to escape. The wealth of the South, based as it was upon cotton and slavery, was at odds from the beginning with the new American nation. The North viewed the South as a foreign country. To restrain the South from extending its way of life into new territories led to the Civil War.

The North tried in vain to contain slavery. Southerners were determined not only to maintain slavery in their homeland but extend it westward: For every free state admitted to the union a slave state also had to be let in. Slave owners got Congress to pass laws mandating that runaway slaves to the North be returned to the South. The United States, in Lincoln's phrase, was a "House Divided."

The Greater Atlanta area became a battleground in the Civil War. During the siege of Atlanta ferocious fighting occurred in all quadrants of the city save the south enabling what was left of the Confederate defenders and Scarlett O'Hara to flee.

Although no major battles were fought in the Indian Fields during the Civil War, the plantation population felt the wrath of marauding raiders of Sherman's march. Food and provisions were commandeered, barns and carriages burned, and the life-style of the Southern gentry smashed.

A war lost is a war never forgotten. It becomes a part of the fabric of being. Future generations remember the conflict as though born with organs transplanted from the fallen heroes.

Sequoyah

Andrew Jackson

(From an original water color by Wilbur G. Kurtz, in collections of Franklin M. Garrett)
Whitehall which became the West End

Pre-Civil War Atlanta

The Atlanta *Constitution* Building

The Piedmont Chautauqua

The Age of Steam

Downtown Atlanta in the 1880s

Almanza Lee, Age 16

Almanza and Ellery Mason

Ellery and Almanza and their children and grandchildren - the year Margaret Mitchell came calling

Ernest

Eva

Ernest and Eva

Henry W. Grady Monument

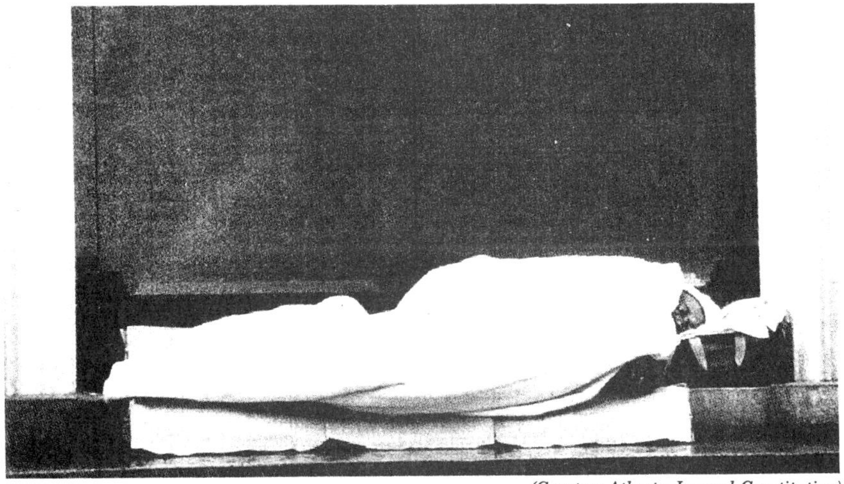

(Courtesy Atlanta Journal-Constitution)

In downtown Atlanta today, Trinity Methodist Church
remains a refuge for the hungry and homeless

Wideman Lee
Father

Ivy Lee
Son

William Burroughs
Grandson

Laura Lee Burroughs

The Three Sisters - Erna, Marguerite (Margie) & Lila

The Author, Cousins Sarah
and Betty, and Sonny

Margie

Jane

Herbert

William Berry Hartsfield

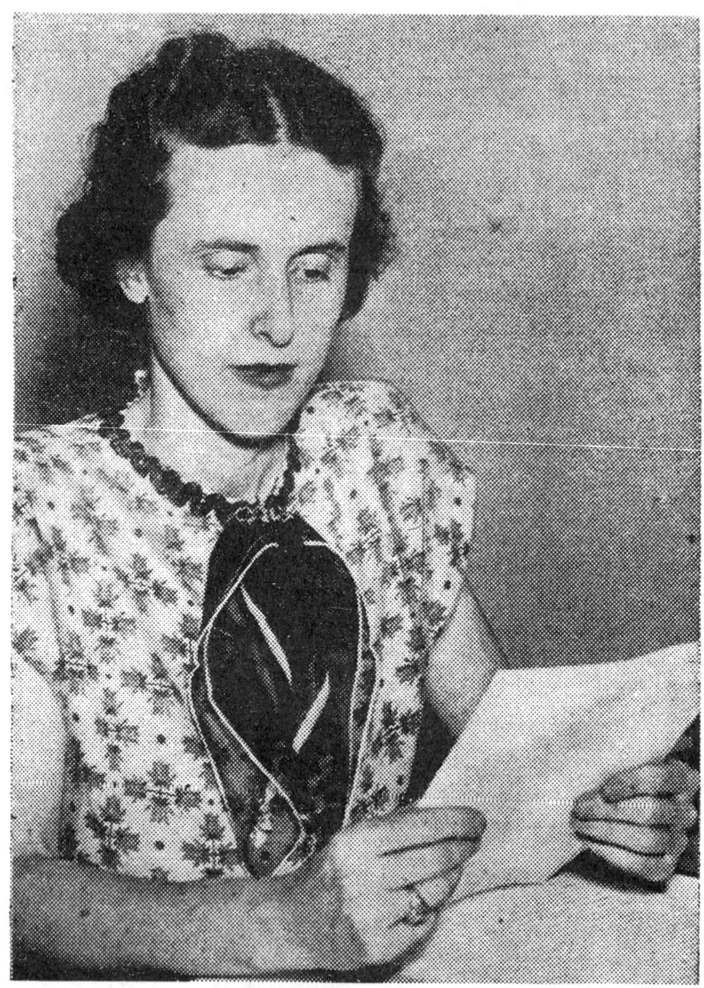

Secretary Must Know What to Do In Whooping Cough, Rabbit Fever

By NANCY BRANYON.

Could you sit calmly at a telephone and tell a very excited mother what to do when her small son catches whooping cough from the little boy down the street?

That's one of the things Miss Erna Mason, secretary to Dr. T. F. Abercrombie, director of the State Health Department, must do in a day's work.

Besides doing her secretarial work and answering the questions of persons who want to know something about any disease from measles to tularemia (rabbit fever to you), Miss Mason helps in the preparation of newspaper articles from the State Health Department which appear every week.

She studied journalism in the University Evening School to know more about how those articles should be written.

This is the first state office that Miss Mason has held, but she's had it for 12 qears, and that should be proof enough she's a very efficient young woman, officials of the department say.

The Atlanta Georgian, August 4, 1937

Scarlet Fever

IN THIS HOUSE

⟷

This Card is Displayed by Order of the Health Department. Any Unauthorized Person REMOVING it is Liable to a FINE of FROM $10 to $100.

FIVE

THE GRADY MONUMENT

Atlanta in the 1880s was like America after the Great Depression. A time of despair followed by vast hope for the future. In both eras a great leader appeared on the scene to reassure and give inspiration to the people. Franklin D. Roosevelt promised Americans a New Deal. Henry W. Grady proclaimed a New South. Both represented turning points in history.

President Roosevelt was the great political leader of his time; Henry Grady was the managing editor of the Atlanta *Constitution*. The former achieved his program via the regular political process being elected president of the United States four times. The latter never ran for elective office and managed "literally to love a nation into peace" as a newspaperman and columnist, brilliant orator, and tireless promoter of the New South and its capital—Atlanta.

The primary emphasis was on rebuilding the very material structure of a society shattered by war and its aftermath. The old order was re-grouping and on the brink of proclaiming Segregation throughout the land. The regular political leadership in such a tumultuous atmosphere merely presided over the inhabitants, and moral and civic advancement became the sole concern of others.

Thus the Media and the Church provided the impetus for change in Atlanta, and the 1880s were an Age of Enlightenment.

The population of the city of Atlanta was 65,000, but some half-dozen newspapers flourished. In their stores and offices, standing on street corners, and seated on front porches, the citizens of Atlanta gorged themselves upon a flurry of printed pages which bombarded them daily.

In the churches on the Sabbath and at countless prayer meetings throughout the week, from the pulpit as well as the press, the theme was hammered home: We in the South, we the sons and daughters of those who fought and died in the war must overcome that defeat and create a New South. The message from all the newspapers and all the pulpits was the same: We were great once and we can be great again. Even though, alas, it shall take a very long time.

Henry W. Grady always knew that his time in this magnificent endeavor would be brief. Born in 1850 in Athens, Georgia, the son of a Confederate veteran, and grandson of a newspaperman, he came to Atlanta in the early 1870s and worked for a number of Atlanta papers before becoming managing editor of the Atlanta *Constitution* in 1876.

Grady was a tornado of energy and involved in every important aspect of Atlanta life in the glorious decade of the 1880s. To bring off a number of expositions, meetings of Atlantans with business leaders of the North, visits from presidents and Northern governors, and promoting Atlanta as the capital city of the New South took a lot of time, money and assistance from others. Like President Roosevelt who managed to institute new programs and reshape America, Grady relied upon a "Brain Trust." He brought together the rising generation of up-to-date Atlantans and molded them into a potent civic force dedicated to enlightenment. The most energetic and forward-thinking of the group became Grady's own brain trust. Of this less than a dozen individuals were those who shown brightest under Grady's tutelage and in turn provided him with the ideas and financial and intellectural support he needed to move Atlanta and the South forward.

The businessmen upon whom Grady most often relied were the Inman brothers: John H. Inman of New York and Samuel H. Inman of Atlanta. His closest scholarly advisor was the Reverend Dr. James Wideman Lee, pastor of Trinity Methodist Church in Atlanta.

Dr. James Wideman Lee, or Uncle Wideman as he was known in the family (he was my mother's great uncle) was but one of a number of protestant ministers who urged racial tolerance, spoke out against anti-Semitism and anti-Catholicism, and preached that in the New South there was room aplenty for both Science and Religion.

Wideman Lee was a gifted author and lecturer who wrote columns for the *Constitution*. He was a well-known figure in his own right but Grady's fame quickly surpassed his own. Lee was born the year before Grady on a large plantation in the Indian Fields. He was an eyewitness to Sherman's March and head of the family as his father was off fighting for the Confederacy when the Yankee troops came looting. Too young to go off to war, he was barely a teenager when the war came to him. Like others of his generation he learned at a youthful age and at first hand about the folly of war.

Wideman Lee's career in Atlanta paralleled Grady's. Not unlike other young people before and after them, they were newcomers drawn to Atlanta because of its central location, importance in the region, and promised them a bright and productive future.

Grady and his brain trust mapped out an agenda to free Atlanta from its old-South past.

Opening in 1881, and going from October to December of that year, the International Cotton Exposition was held at Atlanta's Oglethorpe Park. The Exposition had 1,113 exhibits from all the states of the union and seven foreign countries. Cotton from Mexico, India, and Egypt along with Southern cotton had been planted on the Exposition grounds and was in full bloom opening day.

On Governor's Day (most of the nation's governors being in attendance) a remarkable demonstration was staged at the Exposition. Shortly after sunrise the Georgia cotton was picked and immediately ginned in the model cotton factory which occupied the main building on the grounds. The cotton was woven into cloth and then tailored into suits of men's clothes. By sundown, the completed garments were ready to be worn by the governors during the reception and Governor's Dinner that evening.

The International Cotton Exposition of 1881 had a profound effect upon Atlanta and the South. It highlighted the growing importance of Atlanta as a transportation, distribution, and manufacturing center.

Henry W. Grady was responsible for bringing many of the leading citizens of the United States and prominent business people from abroad to visit the Exposition and as a consequence, Atlanta and the South. When Atlanta was crowded with distinguished visitors, Atlantan's threw open their homes and entertained everyone. It was this seemingly prompt and spontaneous outburst that so impressed visitors to Atlanta that the city gained its reputation of being inhabited by an exceptionally hospitable people. But what appeared as an unplanned manifestation of Atlanta's good manners toward visitors, was actually the many weeks and months of planning on the part of Grady's brain trust.

On those days when he was not out of town on a speaking or lecturing engagement, Wideman Lee would arrive early at his Trinity Church office from his home in the West End. He would tend to church business and around nine if Grady was not out of town or on a tour promoting Atlanta, Wideman Lee would leave his office at the church and go out the back door and walk the three short blocks up Broad Street to Grady's office in the Constitution building. Had he called for his carriage to be made ready and brought around would have created too much commotion and been too time consuming. There was no need to advertise the fact that he was spending time everyday on non-church business, but Widemen Lee and Henry Grady were both young men who could handle many jobs at once. Of course before leaving the church he would don his hat; gentlemen did not venture out-of-doors without wearing a hat. Then too, Grady and Lee and the other members of the brain trust were men who wore many different hats. And it was this custom which gave definition to the decade. Grady and Lee would discuss privately the day's agenda. Later, from varying points in the city, on foot or riding in horse drawn carriages, the other members of the Grady brain trust would converge on the editor's office. It was the daily ritual, and often joining the group would be one or the other—county sheriff, city fire chief and/or police chief, mayor of Atlanta, and governor of Georgia. At these meetings policy for running the city government and the future course of action was debated and decided upon.

For Grady to be able to conduct governmental affairs and put out a paper everyday was a monumental feat. One that has seldon, if ever, been duplicated.

The Exposition of 1881 put Altanta on the map. The Fair was such a hit that it was followed by the Piedmont Exposition of 1887. The Piedmont Exposition was three times larger than the Oglethorpe. The highlight of the Piedmont Exposition was the visit of President Grover Cleveland and Mrs. Cleveland. For the first Democratic President in 24 years to attend an event in Atlanta was the inspiration and work of Grady.

However, the person who Atlantans most wanted to meet and

entertain, was Frances Folsom Cleveland, then the youngest
First Lady in American history, and the bachelor President's recent bride. This was Mrs. Cleveland's first official visit anywhere
as First Lady.

Atlanta went bonkers over Frances Folsom Cleveland. She was
the Jacqueline Bouvier Kennedy of her day. People swarmed
around her carriage whenever she went about, and Atlanta police on horseback barely managed to control the churning
crowds. Certainly she was the first celebrity star to shine upon
Atlanta.

The era of Cotton Expositions came to an end in 1895 with
the Cotton States and International Exposition held at Atlanta's
Piedmont Park. Once again, President Cleveland, who had just
been re-elected president after being out of office for four years,
attended the Fair and marveled at the six thousand exhibits.

The Cotton States and International Exposition was the cul-
mination of the efforts by the South to re-join the Federal union
as equal partners. It showcased to the world that this process
had been achieved. The Exposition attracted nearly One million
visitors and on Atlanta Day 55,000 people (two-thirds of the
city's population) were on the Exposition grounds.

The Exposition contained a Fine Arts Building, Railroad
Building, Agricultural Building, and pavilions housing exhibits
from states of the union and foreign countries. An entire Japa-
nese Village was featured. Buffalo Bill and his Wild West Show
entertained thousands of spectators.

Much more importantly for the future of Atlanta and the
South, the Exposition highlighted something besides cotton and
railroads. It displayed Atlanta's eagerness to be a leader in the
pursuit for equal rights for all Americans.

Prior to the opening of the 1895 Exposition, Susan B.
Anthony came to Atlanta to open the annual meeting of the
American Women Suffrage Association. It was the only time
that organization ever held its annual meeting in the South, for
the Suffragettes had scant membership in the South outside
Atlanta.

Inspired by Susan B. Anthony's visit, a group of Atlanta
women raised $35,000 and erected a Women's Building on the
grounds of the Cotton States and International Exposition. A
woman architect, Elsie Mercer of Pittsburgh, Pennsylvania, was
contracted to design the structure. Upon visiting the Women's
Building, President Cleveland commented that it held more in-

terest for him than any other exhibit.

At that time, women were still denied the vote so obviously the President gained none by praising the Women's Building. Undoubtedly he was impressed by its contents and uniqueness to expositions in that era.

An African-American Building was erected on the Exposition grounds. It was built by an African-American contractor from La Grange, Georgia, and dedicated by Booker T. Washington on opening day.

During the Exposition, when black choirs from all over Atlanta sang, and John Philip Sousa played his *Atlanta* March, Booker T. Washington delivered his famous oration stating that Black people must be a part of the South economically and politically but separate socially as "the fingers of the hand." In this historic speech, Booker T. Washington, accepted Segregation in return for political and economic gain. As it turned out, African-Americans received very little as a result of the "Atlanta Compromise."

But in the last decade of the 19th century, enlightened Southerners hailed the presence of an African-American Building and speeches by Booker T. Washington and other black leaders at the Cotton States and International Exposition in Atlanta in 1895, as heralding great progress in the South in the field of race relations.

Both the Cotton Exposition of 1881 and the Piedmont Exposition of 1887 made money. The big 1895 production, the grandest of the trio of fairs which dominated many aspects of post Civil War life in Atlanta, lost money.

And so, as the century came to a close in Atlanta, so did the century of expositions.

Another endeavor of Henry W. Grady's which expanded the moral consciousness of Atlantans was the Piedmont Chautauqua.

Before Woodstock, before New Wave, even before Channeling, There was Chautauqua. Chautauqua was originally a tent-and-cottage Summer retreat for Methodist preachers and Bible teachers located in the Western-most corner of New York state on the lake of the same name.

Wideman Lee attended one Summer and became an avid Chautauqua enthusiast. As did countless other Americans among them Ulysses S. Grant and Thomas Edison.

When the curriculum was expanded to include study in foreign languages, literature, Science and the Fine Arts during the July through August season, Chautauqua caught on like wildfire and was soon being duplicated all over the country. Chautauqua was the grandparent of the self-help manifestation of our time.

Wideman Lee urged Grady to attend, and although reluctant at first, he agreed to go after others of the brain trust began singing Chautauqua's praises.

Grady returned from his Summer retreat with plans for a Piedmont Chautauqua in Atlanta. As in all other matters Grady passed through the conversion stage and moved right on into the action phase when he thought something was good for the South.

From July 4th to August 28, 1888, Grady's Piedmont Chautauqua was held at a small resort town, twenty miles from Atlanta. Grady did everything. He raised the money from private sources to secure the location, erect the buildings, and brought in faculty from as far away as the University of Virginia to teach classes. From all over the South noted Southerners and just ordinary folk attended the Piedmont Chautauqua.

Henry W. Grady was no wild-eyed reformer but he never ducked a moral issue wherever and whenever it should arise.

Following the lynching of a black man for an assault upon a white girl in a suburb of Atlanta, a mob formed and began attacking and whipping black men at random. Grady wrote a strong editorial condemning the outrages. He received an anonymous letter stating: "Your political aspiration is gone to hell because of your editorial against the attack on the Niggers." Grady published the letter and replied in a two-column editorial:

> "We cannot conceive of a political aspiration so earnest as to interfere with our slightest duty as an editor . . .
> "We cannot expect, and we will not deserve, the confidence of the North, if such outrages go unrebuked and unpunished. Worse than that, we cannot hold our self-respect."

The Young Men's Democratic Club of Atlanta adopted a resolution condemning Henry W. Grady of the Atlanta *Constitution* for his printed opinion. No elected official in Georgia spoke out in defense of Grady.

From his pulpit, Wideman Lee vigorously supported Grady and ringingly denounced random violence.

Henry W. Grady was Atlanta's first national figure. He became a noted personality almost overnight when he delivered his now celebrated "New South" speech in New York City. From that time onward, Grady went about the country making speeches proclaiming a New South. He was trusted by Americans outside the South because he was not a politician, and was not tainted by any association with the South of Jefferson Davis.

In December of 1889, Grady made public appearances in Washington, New York, and Boston. He gave a well-received speech in Boston on the subject of *The Race Problem in the South*. One of his finest orations, it was to be his last; for while in the North Grady caught a cold which had developed into pneumonia by the time he returned to Atlanta. He died December 23. He was thirty-nine years old.

Atlanta and the nation were stunned. Many people felt that on the day Grady died the sun had gone down at noon over the New South. In the judgment of his contemporaries, Grady was a leader of extraordinary promise and more than any other individual expressed the real spirit of the age of which he was regarded as the extreme embodiment. The words most often associated with Grady are as relevant today as when Grady spoke them:

"There was a South of slavery and secession—that South is dead.

"There is a South of union and freedom—that South, thank God, is living breathing growing every hour."

Wideman Lee accepted Grady's untimely death as God's will. The fact that Grady had died young, in Lee's eyes, had put him in the company of Christ. Lee had spent his life as a follower of the latter; now he turned his considerable skill into perpetuating the legacy of the former.

First off, there was the matter of money. Grady had mortgaged his home to make up the Chautauqua deficit. Insofar as Lee had been responsible for Grady's original interest in the Chautauqua Movement, he felt obligated to see that the debt not be a burden upon Grady's widow and two small children. Thus he immediately brought the matter to the attention of Samuel Inman who paid off the debt.

Next, there had to be a fitting and proper memorial in Atlanta to revere Grady's memory. At Lee's urging, a group of Atlanta businessmen formed a monument committee, and Wideman Lee donned his fund-raising hat. This was a talent of his for which he had no equal in the Methodist Church, or for that matter, in Atlanta and Georgia.

Reverend Lee and the brain trust raised $20,000 to erect a monument in Atlanta to honor Grady. Contributions of individuals ranged from ten cents to $1,000 and came from all parts of the country. Lee was determined that donations not come just from Southerners, and expanded the drive to raise money from all sections of the nation. In this endeavor he was aided by citizens of the North who had been moved by Henry Grady's speeches and newspaper columns toward re-uniting a "House Divided." People felt that Grady, second only to Lincoln, had done the most of any American to preserve and perpetuate the American union.

On Wednesday, October 21, 1891, a glorious sun-lit day in Atlanta, the Grady Monument was dedicated. The heroic statue of Grady was cast in bronze and the base of the monument and the pedestal were of Georgia granite. Two female figures, representing "History" and "Memory" flanked each side of the base of the statue. It is one of the most imposing memorials anywhere in the South and is located in Grady Square one block from Five Points in downtown Atlanta.

The monument dedication was the last grand occasion in which horse drawn carriages predominated. In the future, motor cars would be used in Atlanta parades, and the only horses present would be those ridden by police officers working to insure crowd control.

But there was no controlling the ardor of the crowd gathered in Atlanta to honor the city's favorite son. The day before, a group of dignitaries arriving by train from the North, were met and greeted at a junction outside Atlanta and transferred to a special train lavishly decorated with banners to celebrate the occasion. The "monument train" contained a cannon-toting-flatcar which fired off salute after salute hailing the visitors' arrival. There had never before been anything like it in Atlanta.

When the monument train, festooned with red, white, and blue streamers arrived at the main depot in Atlanta, thousands of Atlantans were waiting. They cheered and applauded and set off fireworks. In celebration of the event that part of town was covered-up with carriages and train coaches. At this point in time railroad passenger traffic was at its height and 115 passenger trains along twelve railroad lines passed through Atlanta each day.

Atop the dedication platform on Monument Day people would long remember the governor of Georgia presiding, the governor of New York giving the dedication address, Henry W. Grady's young daughter unveiling the statue of her father, and of the Reverend Doctor James Wideman Lee's invocation.

The invocation, when judged by standards of the time, was not over-long, but it covered a lot of ground and set a high standard for the other speakers.

> "We thank thee for this day, the last and best that has ever dawned . . .
>
> "We thank thee for this day . . . as fair and bright as the life of him in whose memory we raise this monument today . . .
>
> "We lift the day . . . into the light, this monument, that shall commemorate the life and character of one we loved. We place it in the midst of the scenes which he walked and which he loved. *It is the gift of our hearts . . .*
>
> "This stone and this metal embody the gratitude of the people of this entire country. From every hamlet and village and city in this whole nation have come the contributions which here take permanent and enduring form . . .
>
> "As this monument meets the storms and the years of the future may it inspire the same generous impulses, and impel to the same high endeavor awakened by the life of him whose name and fame it bears to coming times . . .
>
> "May it continue to teach the lessons of sacrifice, and earnest work for the public good . . .
>
> "Bless this day the men who worked side by side the noble Grady and wrought for the good of this country in connection with the great newspaper with which his name is forever associated. Guide their hearts and guide their pens. May they help to make real the great visions which he had for his country's good . . .
>
> "Bless this dear Southern land he helped to lift from the dissolution of war and defeat—to *independence* and plenty.
>
> "Bless all the mighty states of this republic he sought at the cost of his life to bring into closer sympathy and love . . .
>
> "May North South East and West be one, as contributions to his memory from all the states as one in this monument."

Speaking out-of-doors, upon a platform in the middle of one of the town's main thoroughfares, surrounded by a multitude of upturned faces, it was the greatest challenge to the speaker in pre-microphone years to make himself heard. During Reverend Lee's invocation the huge crowd was utterly silent. They wished to hear what was said and to do so had to be quiet.

When Lee concluded, the hush which had fallen over the throng when he began, remained. There was noting but silence—then thunderous applause. Reverend Lee was quite abashed. It was not considered proper in those days to applaud prayer. But this was no ordinary day.

The key phrase in the invocation was that which mentioned "Independence." Grady gave the South freedom from oppression from the North, *and* from the tyranny of the Bourbon-ruled slavery-dominated old South. This was the newspaper editor's real legacy.

The Grady Monument, erected in memory of Henry W. Grady, is the only memorial anywhere paid for by public subscription to honor the life and times of a person of the Media.

SIX

COCA-COLA

Anthony Trollope, a prodigious late-nineteenth century novelist, whose mother and brother were well-known writers, often wrote about English clerical life in the mythical cathedral town of Barchester. The rise and fall of clerics of the Church of England and the mechanizations behind the gain and loss of power Trollope chronicles with profound and humorous insight. Had Trollope been writing about Atlanta in the 1890s rather than Barchester he would have had a field day.

It was a time of creation. Alexander Graham Bell invented the telephone. Since death by electrocution was deemed more scientific than hanging, the New York state legislature dismantled its gallows and installed an "electric" chair. A Southern druggist invented Coca-Cola.

In the middle ages alchemists sought to transmute baser metals into gold. The quest for gold stimulated conquest of the Western Hemisphere. In Georgia, the discovery of gold in what is now Greater Atlanta, led to the expulsion of Native Americans.

The new concoction called Coca-Cola, or Coke, was the invention of a chemist. The desire of chemists to delve into the grab-bag of elements of their profession in order to create something new is never ending. In the case of Coca-Cola—another enterprising Atlanta druggist quickly parlayed the new invention into gold.

Dr. John S. Pemberton had quite a flair for developing chemical compounds which he sold in his drugstore for a multitude of illnesses. Along with Coca-Cola he invented Globe of Flower Cough Syrup, Triplex Liver Pills, Indian Queen Hair Dye, Gingerine, Extract of Styllinger, and French Wine of Coca-Ideal

Tonic. Of all these creations none but Coke was destined to really make it big.

Doc Pemberton's over-the-counter medications were first concocted and sold in his drugstore in Columbus, Georgia. When Pemberton moved to Atlanta he opened a drugstore and sold Coca-Cola as a medication for headache and exhaustion. In time, another druggist, Asa Griggs Candler, would become sole owner of Pemberton's creation and make the name Coca-Cola synonymous with Atlanta.

Like Pemberton, Candler hailed from West Georgia. The two men responsible for making Coca-Cola identifiable with Atlanta were from somewhere else. It could be argued that Coca-Cola helped put Atlanta on the map. It could also be argued that newcomers fulfilled that function.

In no time flat, Candler was the richest man in Atlanta. He had come out of nowhere in the post war South to become Atlanta's leading citizen. It had all happened so fast it took the breath away. Atlantans did not know what to think.

The rush, to what would become known to Atlantans as the "soda fountain," to purchase Coca-Cola at five cents a glass, was for many a disturbing development.

Any new invention is looked upon by many people with suspicion. Just because it is new. If the new creation is seen as a threat to the way of life of a people then they will try to ignore it. If that doesn't work, they try to outlaw it. All the churches in Atlanta wanted Atlanta dry. Since Coca-Cola was regarded by many of the church going public as a tonic designed to make life easier for the drinking public, it was a threat. When the school-children of Atlanta began saving their pennies to buy Coke, it had to be outlawed.

By this time Coca-Cola was being bottled and sold nationwide. American youth had embraced the new drink with the fizz with a fervor that a later generation would apply to Rock and Roll music. Decades before Elvis, another phenomenon had popped-open in the American South and foamed-over and drenched a younger generation of Americans.

In Atlanta religious leaders faced a dilemma. Nothing in Atlanta had ever been so overpowering overnight; or so rocked the community. Atlantans were delighted that Coke was bringing recognition to Atlanta. But if drinking Coca-Cola was not in itself bad, it was certainly non-productive. And this was in that time just as great a sin.

Wideman Lee had been transferred to the Methodist church in the West End. There had been a stagecoach community called Whitehall long before there was an Atlanta. But as Atlanta grew so did Whitehall; it became known as the West End and was Atlanta's first suburban community. By the time Wideman Lee had been delegated to the West End to raise money to build a new Methodist church edifice commensurate to the status of the West End of the 1890s, West End had been annexed into Atlanta and an electric streetcar line transported breadwinners every morning into Atlanta and brought them back home again in the evening.

The West End may well have been the premiere/progressive Southern community of the New South prior to the advent of total Segregation. Its tree-shaded streets and Victorian homes and church-on-every-corner topography evoked the quintessence of Southern living. The people had a tolerance for those of different backgrounds and religions.

Emma Eufaula Ledbetter of Cedartown, Georgia, the daughter of a Methodist minister became the wife of Wideman Lee while still a teenager. Her intellect matched her husband's and as a preacher's wife she made her household the center for discussion of public affairs.

Another leading citizen of the West End was Joel Chandler Harris, a writer for the Atlanta *Constitution* and the author of the Uncle Remus stories. Although the most famous, Harris was by no means the only writer in the West End and the neighborhood abounded with poets, artists, and musicians.

Wideman Lee and Harris were longtime friends and both had come of age as members of the Henry Grady brain trust. Lee and his wife were also very close to Mrs. Harris, who was Roman Catholic and one of the founders of the Catholic church in the West End. There were several Jewish families in the West End and African-Americans too. It was a very culturally diverse and intellectually vibrant place to live. In the long Summer evenings the important issues of the day encompassing a wide range of opinion were discussed openly. Musicales echoed in the night-time air. The kids growing up there were exposed to an attitude which placed learning and a high regard for the pursuit of knowledge above all other considerations. Making money was secondary. In fact, the singular pursuit of money was thought at best to be ill-mannered, and at worst, the root of all evil. If you had more money than your neighbors you were extra careful not to flaunt it in the West End. This sentiment was unique. Atlantans were consumed with making money from cotton, railroads, and now—Coca-Cola. The West End philosophy was at odds with the prevailing Atlanta attitude.

Ivy Lee, the eldest son of Wideman Lee, spent his childhood and high school years in the West End, and although he would leave Atlanta and make a name for himself in New York and on the national and international scene, he always stated that his immense success in life was attributable in large measure to the important lessons he learned growing up in the West End.

As an intense youth of fourteen, Ivy Lee was a very interested onlooker the day the Henry Grady monument was dedicated. He marvelled at all the great men present in Atlanta that day and vowed that he would be a great man someday. His father's invocation had a profound effect at least upon one face in the crowd.

That evening, while the visiting dignitaries were being feted at a banquet, another group of Atlantans were meeting at Prohibition Hall to hear an address by Dr. Warren Candler, an up-and-coming Methodist minister who was president of the local Methodist college. Warren Candler was the younger brother of the president of Coca-Cola.

It was a lively meeting in which all the anti-barroom candidates for the city council participated. Reverend Candler gave the principal address of the evening against demon rum. All protestant church folk in Atlanta were campaigning to close all Atlanta barrooms. Prohibition Hall was the meeting place where those working to outlaw alcohol in Atlanta congregated. Reverend Candler gave a stirring address which was interrupted again and again by thunderous applause.

After his address, Warren Candler invited members of the audience to give testimony. All was congenial as speaker after speaker gave personal statements on the evils of alcohol. Then, one participant, after endorsing prohibition, began attacking Warren Candler because the Candler family was selling Coca-Cola. The crowd booed this sentiment.

Then as now the formula for Coca-Cola was a closely guarded secret. Nobody connected with Coke ever spoke publicly of what the "pause that refreshes" was made of. This stance on the part of the company fueled the rumor mills. Even worse, it was becoming common practice for the drinkers of alcohol to chase their whiskey with Coke!! And, horror of horrors, imbibers could be observed on the streets and alleys, mixing their booze with

Coca-Cola! When it became known that Atlanta youngsters had been caught drinking moonshine spiked with Coke, many Atlantans reacted as though the moral fabric of society was on the verge of total collapse.

Whether it was a mere caprice of history, a consequence of time and place, or the logical result of his leadership in other matters, before he had time to reflect upon what was occurring, Wideman Lee was thrust into the forefront of the concern over Coca-Cola.

Not unlike others, in the beginning, Lee had paid scant attention to Coca-Cola, but when he did not encourage his children to drink Coke other West End parents followed his example. Of course, being forbidden made Coca-Cola all that more alluring to kids in the West End. If one of them managed to get possession of Coca-Cola, he would share it with his friends in secret. It became a rite of passage.

Our culture today is so exposed to drugs that in most quarters we have gained both sophistication and knowledge. Not so a century ago. Nobody knew anything about drugs except the chemists. And they weren't talking because if an unlearned public was made aware of what the chemist's concoctions contained, they might be less inclined to swallow these products. That would be bad for business.

The gossip around Atlanta was that Coca-Cola contained a powerful drug native to South America. For the uninformed this put Coca-Cola in the same class as demon rum and should be outlawed. For an educated man like Wideman Lee who counted a number of prominent scientists as friends and colleagues, such an explanation wasn't good enough. He would not be the outspoken critic of Coke until he knew the facts. His attempt to determine what exactly Coca-Cola was made of collided with a stone wall of resistance. Finally, he decided to raise the issue in an open forum.

Toward the conclusion of the annual convocation of Methodist ministers of the North Georgia Conference, Wideman Lee in the very proper phraseology of the day inquired of Warren Candler if it would not be in the public interest for the Coca-Cola Company to disclose the chemical formula of Coke. In a very polite and Christian manner, Warren Candler evaded answering the question. According to an eyewitness who spoke about the confrontation many years later, Lee's questioning of Candler electrified the audience because those present realized even then that the struggle between these two giants of the church concerned more than Coca-Cola. In the words of the eyewitness: "It was like listening to God question Moses and not knowing which was which."

Heeding the advice of Reverend Warren Candler, Coca-Cola began an intense advertising campaign to make drinking Coke a respectable pasttime. Since the youth of America had already embraced Coke completely, it was a lot easier for parents to accept this new intrusion into their daily lives rather than wage a continuing and ultimately losing battle against it.

Warren Candler began an aggressive campaign to put Coca-Cola money to use for the public good. If Atlantans could see that Coca-Cola money was being used to improve the health, education, and moral well being of the citizens, then they would be more inclined to support Coca-Cola. Thus, the pre-eminent institutions in Atlanta in the present day: Emory University, Emory University Schools of Medicine and Theology, and the Woodruff Arts Center owe their existence to Coca-Cola.

At the time when Wideman Lee was dedicating his splendid new church in the West End, Warren Candler had begun the construction of the Wesley Memorial Church Building on the north side of town. Wesley Church was to become more than a church, and from the outset as conceived by Warren Candler was to be a continuing learning center which would promulgate the ideals which the founders of the Piedmont Chautauqua had envisioned. With the death of Henry Grady the Piedmont Chautauqua had passed from the scene. To re-establish this moral influence, the Wesley Memorial Church was founded by Warren Candler, and in time, the outstanding religious and political leaders in the world in the 20th century would speak to overflow crowds at the Wesley Auditorium.

Of course the Wesley Church complex became the center of Methodism in Atlanta and the South and it was financed by Coca-Cola money. This had the effect of placing Coca-Cola in the pulpit and silenced any public rumblings concerning Coca-Cola.

Until the advent of Warren Candler and Coca-Cola, Wideman Lee had been the undisputed leader of Methodism in Atlanta and the South. But clearly he and other members of the Grady brain trust were being overwhelmed by the new Big Fizz on the Atlanta horizon.

The religious and intellectual core of the city which had been headquartered in the West End, now began moving away. The Candler family and others who were becoming rich from the profits of Coca-Cola (there was no federal or state income tax, no tax on corporations, no tax on goods or services, no sales tax and you could become rich in no time and in that sense the 1880s were similar to the 1980s) were moving into the newer and grander suburb of Inman Park on the northeast side of town. Later on, the Coca-Cola barons would move farther northeastward into the grandest of early 20th century Atlanta suburbs: Druid Hills.

Henry Grady had died prior to the Cotton States and International Exposition of 1895, but the exposition was the brainchild and work of the Grady brain trust; but it lost money. It would be the final civic endeavor conceived and carried out in Atlanta by Grady's followers, and the last such undertaking in Atlanta which did not have the full backing and support of Coca-Cola.

In the midst of all this economic, intellectual, and social upheaval the post of Bishop of the North Georgia Conference of the Methodist Church South became vacant, and upon such precipitous and unplanned circumstance does the fate of a people and the plot of a novel of Anthony Trollope turn, and it is to him and other such writers that we must turn to get a glimpse of what is involved in electing a new bishop of the church because then as now the election process is clouded in secrecy.

What is different today is that unless you are personally involved it is not a matter of great importance. In the era when bishops were the megastars of society, everybody cared. Nobody knew just how or exactly who would become the next bishop, but all Atlantans discussed the prospects. Even the ordinary non-churchgoer in Atlanta grasped that it was a contest between Wideman Lee and the brother of the founder of Coca-Cola, Warren Candler. Ironically both saw themselves as the rightful heir to the great legacy left untended since the death of Henry W. Grady.

As family legend would have it, Lee was not only the anointed heir but Grady had predicted that Wideman Lee would one day become bishop and re-unite Southern and Northern Methodists as the crowning achievement of his glorious career. American Methodists had split into separate denominations of North and South over the issue of slavery prior to the Civil War. It was Wideman Lee's great mission in life to work for and bring about re-unification.

But in the ensuing age of racial separation, many Southern Methodists wanted to emphasize *Southern* Methodism and remain separate from the North. Warren Candler, whether by choice or circumstance, became the leader of this group. By remaining a separate entity, these Southern Methodists believed they could better move the South forward; and perhaps they did so. But in the process they also moved Southern Methodistism closer to Segregation.

Since the deliberative process was secret, there is no written record of how the younger brother of the founder of Coca-Cola became Bishop Warren Candler. We do know from the fallout that the selection rocked the church to its foundation. No similar selection ever generated such interest because afterwards Coca-Cola just overwhelmed Methodism in the same way that it overtook Atlanta. Bishop Candler would occupy his post for three decades; Asa G. Candler would serve one term as mayor of Atlanta, and with the profits from Coca-Cola erect a Candler office building, Candler warehouse to store cotton, and a Candler racetrack more grand than any other in the South, until, in fact, the Candlers and Coca-Cola were as one in Atlanta.

For his part, though losing out on becoming bishop, Wideman Lee did not go unrewarded, and he became a presiding elder of the Methodist Church and continued his work of unifying the South and Methodism with the rest of the nation. On the occasion of the 100th anniversary of the birth of Abraham Lincoln, he held a memorial service at Trinity Church—the only such celebration of note held anywhere in the South. The service received wide notice throughout the country.

ATLANTA'S SIGNIFICANT TRIBUTE TO LINCOLN

In the many hundreds of celebrations the country over incident to the centennial of the birth of Abraham Lincoln, there are none which can compare in uniqueness or significance to that which, at Trinity church, in Atlanta, honored the memory of the great American . . .

Perhaps in no other nation of the world, within less than half a century after the extreme bitterness of civil conflict had been implanted in every breast, would such a gathering as this, in tribute to the leader of the conquering armies, be possible . . .

Trinity church was packed to capacity by the veterans of the blue and the gray, their friends and relatives, who gathered to join in this unusual union service commemorating the birthday of Abraham Lincoln . . .

The exercises were decidedly the most interesting ever conceived in this city, and were unique in the annals of Atlanta.

So great was the interest in the service that every seat in the church was taken and several hundred people turned away for lack of space. The Confederate and Union veterans marched into the church together and took seats in front of the pulpit.

Dr. Wideman Lee was selected as the orator for the occasion, and the panegyric pronounced upon the martyred President is one of the finest speeches Dr. Lee has ever made.

A true son of the South, he was not one whit untrue to the man in whose honor the meeting was held . . .

Atlanta Constitution

The Lincoln memorial meeting attracted wide attention and many letters were received by Dr. Lee in regard to it.

My Dear Sir:

I thank you very heartily for the memorial service in Trinity church upon the anniversary of my father's birth. None of the occurrences of last week have affected me so much as this meeting, as an indication of the realization of the hopes which I think guided every act of his while President. It is dramatic that this proof should come from a city destroyed by one of the armies under his command, and be presented by confederate soldiers, listening with approval to an address of such eloquence and patriotic feeling as yours. As his son, I am very grateful for the meeting, and more than grateful for your distinguished part in it.

Very sincerely yours,
(signed) Robert T. Lincoln

During the same week that Wideman Lee gave his memorable speech on Abraham Lincoln, he also preached the funeral for an Atlanta woman whom he had known and worked with on racial and religious matters for many years. The funeral oration attracted wide attention in the press because the pallbearers were all former slaves, or children of former slaves. The fact that both white and black persons participated and attended the service in a non-segregated fashion also became known and forward-thinking Atlantans were made proud. But Klan members and their growing band of sympathizers were outraged. The Klan burned a cross in the dark of the night in Wideman Lee's front yard.

At the next church convocation, Wideman Lee was named pastor of St. John's Methodist Episcopal Church, South, in St. Louis, Missouri. He never again preached another sermon in Atlanta.

But he was not silenced. He preached tolerance and understanding from church pulpits and podiums throughout the United States and abroad, but as he won wide acclaim for his stance on race and religion his influence in the Methodist Episcopal Church South shrank to zero. In the next fifty years in the South, as Segregation dominated all aspects of Southern life, many outstanding Southern liberals would suffer the same fate as Wideman Lee.

The intelligence and energy and force of personality which both Wideman Lee and Warren Candler possessed pushed Atlanta into the 20th century and ahead of other Southern cities. They were both dedicated to the public good, and their foresight still has an enormous impact upon modern day Atlanta. The influence of Coca-Cola as guided by Warren Candler upon health and education in Atlanta and the South has already been noted.

Although many inner-city churches in Atlanta have not survived the wreckers ball (the Wesley Memorial Church was bulldozed in the 1950s to make way for a parking lot) both the West End church and the Trinity church so closely identified with Wideman Lee still play an important role in Atlanta life. Trinity church is the site of the Methodist church's assisting the needy program. Located in the center of old Atlanta across from the state capitol, its bells toll daily to summon the hungry and homeless for food and shelter. No more apt or fitting tribute could better illuminate what the life of a New South Southerner was all about than this church program. It remains a living, thriving, memorial to the spirit and times of Wideman Lee.

Three blocks away, the statue of Henry W. Grady looms large over Grady Square. In the long shadows of Summer the spirits of these two Atlantans often converge, as they did in the days of old, and toil through the night on what the future holds for the old land they dubbed the New South.

While it would be nice to conclude this part of Atlanta's history on a note of universal enthusiasm for the city such was not the case of all those who resided in Atlanta in this period. Two individuals who lived in Atlanta during this time and departed disenchanted were a future president of the United States and the founder of the National Association for the Advancement of

Colored People. Woodrow Wilson practiced law in Atlanta for a while but left because he did not think he had much of a future in Atlanta. William E.B. DuBois was a college professor in Atlanta until Segregation began overtaking the city. All of which proves that no matter how enlightened a period in the history of a city, it cannot accommodate the intellectual development of all individuals or endure for longer than the best and brightest of its citizens can manage to grow and perpetuate new ideas.

SEVEN

HANDS

It is not generally realized that the cotton-growing South boomed in the latter half of the 19th and first two decades of the 20th century.

We get too caught up in the matter of Reconstruction, Segregation, and Share-Cropping. For those who were able not to get caught up in any of these tumultuous events, the steady Southern farmer, both Black and White, was making it economically as well if not better than they had before the war. Cotton-growing conditions weatherwise were near perfect, and there was an enormous demand for cotton worldwide. The Industrial Revolution, although mostly bypassing the Southern United States, had an insatiable appetite for the region's foremost export.

The plantation families of the Indian Fields had to face up to the new reality. Some, those with the largest acreage, departed. They found it impossible to maintain their plantations without the ready availability of slave labor. Many of the younger generation like Wideman Lee would ultimately move to Atlanta.

Major Zachry Lee, the father of Wideman Lee, survived the Battle of Gettysburg and was granted leave to return to his Georgia plantation. While on leave he was engaged in winemaking and at about dark he kept urging his young daughter, Almanza, to come closer with the kerosene lantern. As she did so she accidentally got too close and the alcohol in the wine ignited and flamed-up upon her father's wine-spattered clothes and he was fatally burned. His young daughter was not injured physically but badly wounded psychologically, and for the remainder of her long life she blamed herself for her father's untimely death.

When she grew to young womanhood Almanza married Ellery

Mason whose family also resided in the Indian Fields. She literally married the boy next door. Ellery Mason was the same age as Alamanza Lee's older brother, Wideman, and they had been friends since childhood. Both had front row seats along Sherman's *March to the Sea*, and both realized the folly of the Civil War.

Although the Lees along with most of the other families of the Indian Fields were slave owners, the Masons were not and Ellery was spared the trauma of having much and losing much and needing years of inertia and soul searching to recover from the loss, and despite the social and economic upheaval of the times Ellery just kept on doing what his forefathers before him had done: He planted cotton, chopped cotton, picked cotton, and baled cotton without ever missing a beat. As a result, he became country rich—he ended up owning many of the plantations of the Indian Fields.

Almanza Lee Mason, between the ages of nineteen and thirty-six, had nine children, two girls and seven boys, all of whom would live into their eighties and nineties. Not to lose an offspring in childbirth in the South during this time or from childhood disease was a rarity, and to have many sons to work the cotton fields was an added blessing for which both Almanza and Ellery gave thanks daily to all-mighty God. Although they prayed to the same God Almanza, like all the Lee's, was a Methodist and Ellery was Baptist: A very firm kind of Baptist. No drinking, no dancing, no card playing, and no working on the Sabbath. Even though Almanza had grown up in a much more socially liberal household, she readily accepted her husband's stern way of living. It was in some way atonement for the part she felt she played in her father's death.

Ellery, who served as Justice of the Peace in the Indian Fields, had a talent for cotton farming, and his own family work force to carry out the farm chores. A family of girls would have been a disaster for a guy like Ellery because in the after-war South you had to have "Hands" to help you grow cotton on a large scale and do the work previously done by slaves. You could hire hands, employ Sharecroppers, but this was costly because all the desirable hands would have families to care for and therefore needed higher wages.

Southern women had worked the cotton fields during the time when the menfolk were away fighting the Civil War, but as soon as the war ended, male domination of the agricultural society was quickly re-imposed. Slaves had been freed by the war; but not women. Women had shown they could do the work during the war, but were not allowed to do so afterward. No self-respecting Southern planter would allow his womenfolk to work in the fields, save at cotton-picking time when everybody had to pitch in to bring in the crop.

From my own time much later, when I would come to spend the Summer in Ellery's and Almanza's old homeplace, one of my earliest memories of grown up conversation was about hands. So the subject of hands was much on my mind as a youngster. And not just the men who were hired to work on the farm, but the kind with five fingers. I would stare by the hour at a picture of Ellery and Almanza taken during mid-life by a passing traveling photographer as they posed amid the background of their flourishing fields. They stood there, ramrod straight, and I realized from their expressions that they were happy and well pleased with their successful life together: Almanza with her hands folded in front of her and Ellery holding her arm they were a picture perfect vision of Southern life of the period and it was hard to realize that it was a photograph of another time until my eyes gazed upon their hands and I understood with a jolt that they had lived at a time when everything had to be done by hand and after a lifetime of doing everything by hand, your hands showed the wear and tear of always having been used to do whatever had to be done.

In a pre-automated world, the work of an agricultural lifetime comes to fruition in the hands. Only in third world countries do such hands exist in the present day.

EIGHT

FAMILY PHYSICIAN TO BIG BUSINESS

On their rare visits to Atlanta—they made a special trip to the city just to hear Wideman Lee's oration on the 100th anniversary of the birth of Abraham Lincoln and Almanza thought it a splendid occasion and she delighted in seeing all the people in Atlanta who had such a high regard for her brother and although Ellery thought it very appropriate to honor Lincoln he didn't see why it had to be such a big to do social occasion and he was amazed at the number of motor cars on the streets since his last visit and he remarked to Almanza that all the people driving about certainly were in a hurry to get where they were going and he wondered if they knew where they were going— they would go and visit with the Wideman Lee family in the West End. When their children came to Atlanta they would stay with their Lee cousins and came to think of the Lee home in the West End as their home away from home.

After the Wideman Lee family moved to St. Louis, Almanza and Ellery had scant reason to journey to Atlanta. This suited Ellery just fine because Atlanta had become a place of too much hustle and bustle to suit him.

In spite of his demanding schedule Wideman Lee thought of Almanza often and always had concern for her welfare because she was the only member of the family who lived in the Indian Fields, who still knew the everyday harshness of that life but also its serenity of tempo which he undoubtedly at times longed for.

PASTOR'S STUDY
Saint John's M.E. Church South
Saint Louis, Missouri

Dec. 21, 1912

My Dear Sister Almanza;-

I drop you this line to say "Happy Christmas" to you and the family. I sent you a check the other day asking you to buy for yourself a Christmas present of some kind. I hope that you received it.

In many of your letters you write me about the plantations your good husband is buying. You tell him to hold up on the plantations a while now and enjoy his money during the rest of his life. I wish you and Ellery would come out and pay us a visit and see the Mississippi River and the great city of St. Louis. It would do you both good. It would be better for you than a new plantation. Ellery has got ample to keep him comfortable without another lick of work, and if I were him I would learn how to enjoy what I had earned and saved by hard labor.

With all good wishes to you and the family, I am

Affectionally yours,

James Wideman Lee

Ivy Lee, who was a special favorite of Almanza's, also wrote to her and visited in the Indian Fields when he was in Georgia.

Ivy Lee had graduated from Princeton where his Political Economy professor had been Woodrow Wilson with the idea of becoming either a lawyer or journalist. He became neither. Instead he was a pioneer in an absolutely new field of endeavor: He was the first *public relations* man in America.

Our world today is filled with marketing specialists, creative directors, public relations experts, press agents, press secretaries, media flacks and damage control operators. It seems that every aspect of life in America has its own team of interpreters bombarding us daily with what their business or organization or periodical or movie is all about. The rapid increase in the communications industry makes it necessary for an army of people to follow a career in the profession of explaining to us what is going on on the planet. What it now takes an army to do the job in the not too distant past was handled by one man. Ivy Lee was the father of ballyhoo.

But he would be much chagrined to have himself so portrayed.

64

He regarded the Art of Public Relations to be a high calling to which he applied every scintilla of intelligence he could muster to place in the most favorable light the moguls of industry and the business firms they headed in the era of America's Gilded Age.

From his office, which occupied the entire 34th floor of a New York City skyscraper, Ivy Lee represented the largest companies in America. Big business was his client. Beginning with the Pennsylvania Railroad in 1908 he was engaged "to interpret the Pennsylvania Railroad to the public and interpret the public to the Pennsylvania Railroad."

Ivy Lee saw himself as a "family physician to big business." He believed the relationship between business interests and the public could be smoothed by explanation and an honest statement on the part of business and what they were about.

Until Ivy Lee's time American business had a "the public be damned" attitude which was characteristic of the Gilded Age. Since the railways at the time were under continuous attack Lee insisted they must adopt new tactics if they were to have a better public image. He induced many reforms in the railroad's dealings with the press and public and when he went on to represent other giants of industry like Standard Oil and Bethlehem Steel he became a virtual spokesman for the business interests he represented. When any of the moguls of the day got into trouble their first response was "to get Ivy Lee."

But it was in 1914 when Colorado miners struck the Colorado Fuel and Iron Company owned by the Rockefellers, and Ivy Lee took over the public relations of the entire Rockefeller family and continued as their spokesman throughout the remainder of his life, that he became one of the great figures of the age. Indeed, the only Atlantan before him to move in such rarefied circles had been Henry W. Grady.

In his handling of John D. Rockefeller's public image he realized that his idea that big business best could defend itself from bitter press attacks by an attitude of complete frankness had to be expanded upon. When it became known that eleven children and two women had suffocated in a cave where they had fled the gunfire between striking Colorado miners and armed guards of Rockefeller's company in which several miners also were either killed or wounded, the Rockefeller family became the most hated family in America, the archsymbol of ruthless capitalism run amok.

Ivy Lee advised John D. Rockefeller, Junior, to go to Colorado and negotiate with the striking miners himself because contrary to what his Colorado managers were telling him there was a lot more than union agitation behind the strike.

John D., Jr., took his advice and went to Colorado and met with the striking miners, surveyed the living conditions of their wives and children, and ultimately negotiated a settlement which enhanced the livelihood and quality of life of the miners and their families. When the younger Rockefeller was photographed dancing with one of the miner's wives at a celebration party, Ivy Lee made sure the photograph found its way into newspapers all over the world.

Ivy Lee urged John D. Rockefeller, Senior, to come out of seclusion, mingle with the press and the public, and get himself photographed handing out shiny new dimes to little children.

But Ivy Lee's greatest achievement was in the worldwide fame he helped bring to Rockefeller as the greatest philanthropist of all time. He insisted that after the Colorado settlement that Rockefeller philanthropies to the underprivileged be vastly increased. Overnight the Rockefeller prestige, which had plummeted to rock-bottom, began to climb. Newspapers that once derided John D. Rockefeller, Senior, now began extolling the Rockefeller family's good works.

Boys and Girls clubs, public works, conservation projects, restoration of historic sights including the entire city of Williamsburg, Virginia—anything to improve the life of the citizenry and beautify the nation were supported by the Rockefeller family, as were Protestant, Catholic, and Jewish charities.

In Atlanta, Spelman College, an institution of higher learning for African-American women, and named after Laura Spelman Rockefeller wife of John D., Senior, greatly benefited from the Rockefeller largess because Wideman Lee urged his son not to forget the old home town when the gravy train left the station.

Throughout the 1920s Ivy Lee became an advisor not only to American companies but foreign business as well. But he never entirely forgot where he came from. By a strange twist of fate, the Coca-Cola Company became one of his accounts in the twenties when he advised Coke on doing business in the mid and far East and Russia. The irony of that is further compounded by the fact that the advice Ivy Lee gave John D. Rockefeller was the exact same advice which Warren Candler had given Asa Griggs Candler but a decade previous.

Soon after his son had become world famous, Wideman Lee died at his post in St. Louis. He had lived long enough to see his son become far more famous than himself. He had also lived long enough to see to his dismay Segregation and Anti-Semitism gain a strong foothold in America. His heart if not his person never left Atlanta, and his concern for the city's future was always on his mind. The following is a copy of a letter he wrote to Governor John Slaton of Georgia, who, years before, had served as chairman of the board during Lee's pastorate at Trinity church. It concerns the infamous Leo Frank case.

Leo Frank who was Jewish, had been convicted of murdering a young white Protestant girl who was employed at the pencil factory in Atlanta where Leo Frank was her boss. There was considerable doubt in Atlanta and throughout the nation of Frank's guilt. Many enlightened people of the day urged Governor Slaton to pardon Leo Frank. Among them was Wideman Lee.

Saint Louis, Missouri
June 12, 1915

My Dear John:-

I cannot begin to tell you how often you have been in my thoughts and prayers these past two weeks. How I wish that I could be there to offer you solace in this terrible hour of your destiny.

Ivy sends me clippings on the Frank case from all the important newspapers and I must tell you that it just tears at our hearts. It sometimes seems that all we have worked so hard to achieve will be lost, but I pray that this will not be the result. My sense tells me that this hardship too shall pass.

We are all so prayerfully thankful that the case rests with your undoubted strength of conscience which with God's Grace I was able to rely upon so many times over the long years of our close Christian friendship, and we know that whatever the cause, whatever the concert of the moment, and whatever the life we must all lead until we walk into the outstretched arms of our Lord and Master that we shall make that unblemished journey as one with God, our Father in Heaven.

We know, as few others know, that during all your public life you have had at your side a wife who is as one with the angels and who has been God's greatest gift to you always.

67

We pray for the both of you—and for deliverance.

Prayerfully Yours,

James Wideman Lee

On June 21, 1915, Governor John Slaton commuted the death sentence of Leo Frank. Rioting broke out in Atlanta and Governor Slaton was saved from bodily harm by local police and firemen and the Georgia National Guard that fought off marauding bands of crazies who attempted to enter the governor's home and seize Governor Slaton. Leo Frank was not so fortunate. A mob overcame guards and took Frank from jail and lynched him. When his term as governor was concluded, Slaton had to live many years outside of Georgia for his own safety. Like Wideman Lee he too became an exile.

With the death of Wideman Lee, Ivy Lee's only remaining link with his father's Southerness was through Aunt Almanza. He sent her books and newspaper articles and copies of letters covering his life and career in the wider world far removed from the everyday life in the Indian Fields.

Ivy Lee was twenty-eight years old when he made the first of what would be many trips to Europe and Russia. He made contacts with individuals in Russia who ultimately came to power following the Communist revolution, and represented Western business interests that continued trading with Russia throughout the turmoil. He also had clients in China and Japan and continued to do work for some of the largest European cartels. With the rise of fascism, his work in Europe brought him into serious conflict.

While on a train crossing the Steppes of Central Asia on his way to Vladivostok and then on to an international conference in Kyoto, Japan, American newspapers broke the story that Ivy Lee represented German companies controlled by Nazis. Upon his return to the United States he was summoned before a congressional committee to explain why he received $25,000 a year from a German dye trust within three months after Adolf Hitler came into power as German chancellor.

The inference of the investigation was that Ivy Lee was acting as a propagandist for the German Nazi interests. Lee insisted he was under attack because all his life he had been an internationalist and all his accusers were isolationists. Any advice he had given the Germans merely as a public relations expert regarding

68

their relations with the United States was as much in the interest of Americans as Germans. Ivy Lee had his eldest son posted in Germany, and when he reported back that the Nazis had murdered the chief of police of Berlin, Lee immediately severed all contacts with Germany.

Clearly Ivy Lee had been taken in by the Nazis, and although others such as Charles Lindbergh had been similarly misled, there were those who took great delight in the fact that the inventor of public relations had himself fallen victim to propaganda.

Ivy Lee was staggered by these attacks upon his character and integrity and really had a difficult time grasping how it all came about. Was it merely carelessness? Had he been too busy to see quickly what the Nazis were up to? Or had he just been greedy? The latter, of course, being a far worse lapse in ethical behavior. Or perhaps had he simply become out-of-date—that the mechanism he devised to correct the excesses of 19th century capitalism was no longer relevant as the 20th century moved onward? Whatever the cause, he was determined to redeem his good name.

Whereas before his work had been merely a career it now became a crusade. Artfully avoiding any foreign company that had any totalitarian connection, he continued to give advice to businesses and governments on how they should present themselves to the world. After an extensive and exhausting whirlwind tour, he met with FDR in the Oval Office and gave the president his assessment of the world situation. Shortly afterwards, he collapsed at a meeting in New York and died in 1934 at the age of fifty-seven. An autopsy showed he had a massive brain tumor. Many people felt the attacks on his character is what really killed him.

Although his name is forever linked with the richest people in America, Ivy Lee did not die a wealthy man. He could have because he earned vast sums (he never sent a bill and always accepted whatever payment his client thought his services were worth) but spent even vaster sums on the support personnel and travel that he felt was an absolute requirement in the conduct of his endeavors. Then too, much of his advice to individuals as well as governments was free. He was also a soft touch: virtually an entire generation of impecunious Southern relatives achieved college educations thanks to his ongoing generosity.

The legacy of Ivy Lee continued long after his death. No college student in Lee's field of work would graduate without studying the career and methods of Ivy Lee. Many individuals now regard him as the ultimate professional of the golden age of press agentry.

In fact the influence of three generations of this family upon American life is incalculable: Wideman Lee, his son Ivy Lee, and his grandson William Burroughs. Burroughs, author of *Naked Lunch*, parent of the Beat generation, herald of the counter-culture which blossomed in the 1960s, has been, in some quarters, characterized as the end product of too much 19th century Methodist do-goodism. Certainly the swing in the pendulum within this amazingly rampant American family of the deepest Southern roots which tolled changes in the 20th century has affected modern life in a variety of ways.

It appears to have come about as a blending of what non-Southerners would dub as eccentricism into the mainstream of American civilization. Which stated in reverse translation means that: Three generations of this family could only be the creation of William Faulkner.

All of which seems to prove that while the worst of Southernism as personified by the Ku Klux Klan could not permanently thrive in America, other, more positive contributions as those made by three individuals in succeeding generations of this Southern family are an essential part of the fabric of that multifaceted creation we call an American.

NINE

OH MARGARET, WHAT TOOK
YOU SO LONG?

The South was once again on the verge of being invaded by an aggressor that would ultimately reek more havoc in Georgia than Sherman.

The boll weevil, a small beetle which has destructive larvae that hatch in and destroy cotton bolls, was discovered in 1910 in Texas. Experts predicted that within ten years time the boll weevil would be in Georgia. Skeptics said that the experts were wrong, that the boll weevil would never make it across the wide Mississippi River. But they were the ones who were wrong.

By the time of World War I, the boll weevil was destroying crops in Alabama and, as the experts predicted, hit Georgia cotton fields in 1920. Farmers left Georgia farms in droves and headed for Atlanta. Those who stuck it out on the farms had to learn to diversify.

By the time old boll weevil reached Ellery's spread in the Indian Fields, he was ready for him. He had begun converting to other crops and planting many of his fields in fruit trees. The glory days for growing cotton in the South was fast coming to a close and Ellery realized it and didn't waste anytime fretting over its passing. Of course growing corn and sugar cane did not produce the kind of revenue King Cotton generated, but at this stage in his life Ellery and Almanza were content not to work so hard and enjoy long visits from their many grandchildren.

One blissful Summer afternoon a touring car loaded with Lee relatives arrived to visit their Aunt Almanza. Among them was the beautiful Laura Lee, the youngest sibling of Wideman Lee who had few memories of the South she had departed at an early age. She was engaged to be married to the son of a well-to-do St. Louis family and was being feted by her Southern kin prior to her marriage and had come to visit briefly with her father's favorite Southern relative.

For those young granddaughters who had been plucked from their outside playtime pursuits and forced to bathe and put on their Sunday best for the occasion, they had been at first resentful, but then completely won over by the appearance in all her Summer finery of the very personable and well-brought-up, Laura Lee. They talked of nothing else but the visit for the remainder of the Summer, for it was the highlight of their lives. They all swore they would grow-up to be as beautiful and fashionable as Laura Lee. This cousin from the wider world had become their ideal. They wanted to be like her. They peppered Grandma Almanza to tell them any details she learned from letters on the doings of this fabled relative.

Laura Lee married and had two sons, the youngest being William Burroughs. She became a writer also and turned out a number of books on flower arranging. Several of these books were published by the Coca-Cola Company.

But Ellery never took Wideman Lee's advice to travel. Neither he nor Almanza ever ventured far from the Indian Fields or set foot outside of Georgia. They were genteel country folk and were quite happy being who they were, and saw no need to go off traveling in search of a wider identity.

As the roaring twenties came to a close and Ellery and Almanza were nearing the end of their lives, many folks visited them and shared the news of family and friends and country life. Ellery had served on the school board for many years and had been instrumental in bringing public education to the Indian Fields. He had given up his Justice of the Peace job because he and Almanza had become too old to be roused at all hours of the night to accommodate young folks wanting to get married.

But even so, Ellery remained the senior esquire, the elder statesman of that part of the county, for, when others had fled, he held onto his lands and prospered despite war, defeat, and Reconstruction. He was a survivor.

As the well-known surviving planter of the area, it was only natural that individuals interested in the South's past would come and seek him out. One young woman from Atlanta much interested in writing about the true South made several visits to interview Ellery and Almanza concerning life in the Indian Fields during the time of Sherman's March.

The reign of the cotton princesses is now long gone. She was a fixture in the South in the first half of the century. She ruled at debutante balls, rode on the floats in a thousand King Cotton parades, and was relentlessly pursued at football-crazy Southern colleges and universities by whatever sorority lucky enough to pledge her and the much envied fraternity brother lucky enough to pin her.

But even in her heyday she was a monument to the past. The last remaining link to the much ballyhooed cotton-culture hype.

The author of *Gone With The Wind* was of the generation of the cotton princesses. Although she presented a facade of cotton-white appearance, her innards were of a hardier manufacture. Her mother had been a suffragette and Margaret Mitchell lived in Atlanta, a city girl born and bred. She had gone to college in the North shortly after World War I and come of age in the roaring twenties.

As the quintessential flapper the author of *GWTW* had done quite a lot of roaring in her youth. As she grew older she became more serious and began a life-long quest to define the modern woman and discover what made her tick. Margaret Mitchell's method of understanding herself and evoking feminism was to rediscover the past.

Onto the red earth of Western Gwinnett County Georgia long before there was an Atlanta thirty miles farther west had come the English-speaking settlers. They entered upon this land in the early 1800s just as the Native Americans were exiting. One family of incoming white folks having fled oppression and hunger in the old world called their new home in the Indian Fields the Promised Land.

The outgoing Indians wept as they embarked from *their* promised land as they began their journey westward. Africans had been taken from their own promised land and brought by force to work in the Southern cotton fields. Whether or not you view a land as *the* promised land, depends upon whether you are coming or going.

As the white settlers before her, Margaret Mitchell came to the plantation the inhabitants had called Promised Land. She hoped the plantation would do for her in her time what it had done for them in their time.

The Promised Land plantation adjoined the Lee plantation

and lands which Ellery ultimately acquired. It was one of the largest spreads in the Indian Fields and a platoon of slaves worked its furrows. The squire of the Promised Land plantation had laid claim to 800 acres of prime-growing cotton land, and he was the most energetic plantation owner of the era. Opposed to secession mania and then war, he had kept a meticulous farm journal from the year he arrived at his Promised Land. By the time of the Civil War he had become an extraordinary observer of the people and events of the day. His words and anger during the years of Secession, Civil War, and Reconstruction crackle across the pages of his terse and feisty reporting.

Margaret Mitchell read and re-read the unpublished farm journal in a dimly lit room of the Atlanta Historical Society. The journal had found its way into the hands of the society for safe keeping after the old planter's death and his descendants had fled the war ravaged former confederacy.

Traveling the red-rutted roads of Western Gwinnett County in the days of the boll weevil invasion, Margaret Mitchell began her quest. She found the old promised land plantation home in faded yet well-kept repair. It had changed little in appearance since the days when a raiding party from Sherman's March had laid waste to the site, burning the barn and the gin piled high with cotton.

With something of a start, Miss Mitchell realized, however, that the residents had changed; for the plantation, once the center of activity in the slave economy of the Indian Fields, was now owned and occupied by Robert and Morena Livsey and their children, an African-American family. For an enterprising few, the Civil War had changed things.

Across the river, was what had been the plantation where the aristocratic brother-in-law (who many people believe was the basis for the character Ashley Wilkes in *GWTW*) of the author of the farm journal resided, and was still in ownership by this same family. Margaret Mitchell knew she had found the perfect plantation house for her family of fiction, the O'Hara's, to inhabit in her yet untitled novel. Thus Tara, named after the home of the ancient kings of Ireland, was born.

Of course Margaret Mitchell always insisted that Tara was a fictional place but if you are familiar with the brother-in-law's house as depicted in the farm journal, and then read the opening sections of *GWTW* you realize how heavily Margaret Mitchell relied upon the farm journal not only for recalling the times and lives and manners of a Southern plantation household prior to the Civil War, but also the actual layout and floor plan of the house itself, and even the mention in *GWTW* of the fact that a smaller house on the Tara site which burned is also taken from the farm journal. What the author of *GWTW* did was portray a plantation of the Indian Fields and move it to the area south of Atlanta where the action of her novel takes place. A plot creation no one would have ever known about had not so many people she interviewed in the Indian Fields told over time their children and grandchildren of her many visits to Gwinnett County and to the brother-in-laws' house in particular.

Being off the main road, the Gwinnett County Tara did not sustain as much damage by Sherman's raiders as other Georgia plantations. When paved roads entered the region, it was by-passed once again. No outsider could ever find it without local help.

During my Summers in the Indian Fields everybody referred to the brother-in-law's house as Tara, and when you saw it, it was the same as all the world knew from the pages of *GWTW*.

The house was built of brick made from red mud and the roof of the front veranda was supported by four columns of mud bricks and whitewashed. There was so much rock and timber available in North Georgia that brick houses were rare. That one survived intact until the late 1920s made it unique.

When the movie makers filmed *GWTW* they constructed on a Hollywood back lot a facade of Tara to be shown in *GWTW*. When the viewer first sees Tara in the film it looks exactly as the view from the bend in the road of the brother-in-law's plantation as taken from the pages of *GWTW*, and unmistakenly identifies the brother-in-law plantation as Tara. What the world has come to think of as a typical ante bellum Southern plantation in the land which had previously been Indian country, is an aberration. Had Mitchell wanted to portray a typical plantation house of the time and place she would have made the Promised Land plantation house Tara. It was two-story, constructed of solid heart pine, and had massive rock chimneys on either side. It still stands today. The South in the period was filled with such houses.

What the Promised Land house lacked was columns. Oh, it had four squat four-by-fours holding up the front veranda, but that was it. Mitchell was wise enough to know that any novel about the old South had to have houses with massive and impressive columns. This the brother-in-law house had, and its whitewashed columns shining in the Southern Summer sun looked just like a Southern plantation *ought* to look. Mitchell was ecstatic. She knew readers of Southern novels expected hen houses to have columns; so, the fictional Tara could have columns and be authentic: She had seen the house standing with her own eyes. Nobody thought it important enough to tell her that the house was an architectural freak.

Thus, an unreal house of its time and place, is moved into a real place, fictionally speaking, and is made famous by a writer who claims that Tara is not a real house which nevertheless becomes in peoples minds' the most real Southern house ever constructed!!

In the 1930s the white brick house was covered with wood siding; the crumbling brick columns replaced with traditional wooden ones.

On a return visit to the Indian Fields prior to the filming of *GWTW*, Margaret Mitchell was pleased to discover her supposedly fictional Tara had been entombed. Now without fear of contradiction she could tell one and all that Tara was a place that did not exist.

Neither Ellery or Almanza lived long enough to read *GWTW* or view the movie. In the last years of their lives the aging couple sat on their front porch holding hands—cooing like lovebirds and watching their grandchildren playing under the magnolia tree.

All the young granddaughters felt themselves to be so lucky to visit in a household where there was so much love, and all vowed to have a marriage someday on a par with that of Ellery and Almanza; but few succeeded. Not because they did not try but because in a world beyond the time of the generation of their grandparent's, it was so much more difficult to do so, for the patterns of partnership no longer fit the persons who lived in the South when cotton was no longer king and his princess was nothing more than a beauty queen floating down Peachtree Street to the accompaniment of the Georgia Tech Marching Band playing Dixie.

TEN

THE ENGINE THAT WOULD

At the southern terminus of the Indian Fields was the town of Lithonia. Located on the Georgia railroad, it was the departure point for travel to Atlanta and Augusta, and the shipment of cotton to the North and to coastal seaports and ultimately to overseas markets.

The town of Lithonia, an important railroad stop in its day, was built on underlying granite beds, and there were more extensive granite outcroppings here than anywhere else in north Georgia thus the name derived from the Greek word, lithos, meaning stone.

English-speaking settlers mostly of Scots and Welsh descent came to the area and secured employment as stonecutters. These artesians fashioned the stone from three granite mountains in the Lithonia area into Belgian-block which was loaded onto railroad cars and shipped via the Georgia railroad to Atlanta. The first permanent street surfaces in the city of Atlanta were paved with these blocks and countless numbers of stores and residences in the city were built, if not entirely of Lithonia granite, had solid stone foundations.

My paternal grandfather's family had come from Wales in the early 19th century and homesteaded on Lithonia lands once sacred to the Creek Indians. In time, they prospered and built the Arabia Mountain-Lithonia Railroad. This seven-mile small gauge track railroad connected with the Georgia railroad in Lithonia and transported Belgian-block from Arabia Mountain to the main line and then onto Atlanta.

Long before my time this tiny railroad was huffing and puffing along the rugged Lithonia terrain trying to keep up with the ever increasing demand for the region's granite of the growing city of Atlanta. I've always envisioned the railroad and its mini-bus-sized engine as "the little engine that could," for such a small engine had to constantly haul heavily-laden cars at a fast clip.

In the heyday of the Arabia Mountain railroad when orders for Belgian-block would pile up it became necessary for the railroad to operate from sunrise to sunset seven days a week. To labor on the Sabbath was a great sin, and insofar as the railroad rocked and rolled within fifty yards of the local Methodist church, the minister became enraged and called down God's vengeance upon the Arabia railroad as its banging and clacking and whistle blowing infringed upon the tranquility of the Lord's Day.

One busy Sunday morning as the little engine that could was working diligently along its track, the preacher once again prayed for help from upon high that this desecration of the Sabbath be at an end. And it was.

Just as the little engine chugged an extra heavy load along the track near the church, and, just as the fireman was stoking the fire, the boiler blew-up and the little engine detonated into hundreds of pieces of hot metal that witnesses said showered down upon the landscape like the fires of hell. The two men on board the train, the engineer and the fireman, were both killed. Too small for the demands made upon it, the Arabia Mountain railroad was abandoned, and, replaced by a full spur track of the Georgia railroad, and since the new line could transport much larger loads with fewer runs along the line, the new train never had to operate on Sundays.

Arabia Mountain, although vastly reduced in size because of the granite-cutting operations conducted upon its surface, remained a formidable sight upon the Lithonia landscape. The family farm adjoined Arabia Mountain and the railroad access to it. The children in the family played along the track and upon and around the mountain. One day when they were outdoors trying to scare each other playing cowboys and Indians, one of the kids ran to hide behind a large granite boulder and almost collided with a tall adult who was a stranger in the area. The kid's mouth fell open in surprise and for a moment he was frozen in terror and could not speak until finally he managed to shout the word "Indian! Indian!" again and again as he and all the other children ran into the house.

Yes indeed, the stranger was a real Indian, come from the

West to visit the shrine that had been the sacred mountain to his ancestors. The fact that the new people on the block were cutting up and selling off this ancient monolith did not seem to faze him; he was just glad to have finally reached the end of his long pilgrimage. He stayed on the family farm for several months and took odd jobs around town to pay for his keep. When he had no work he entertained the children with stories about the way life was in this place that he had heard about from his people of the time before the white man came.

When the boll weevil arrived at the same time that demand for Lithonia granite waned because Atlanta streets were being smoothed over with newer man-made pavements, my paternal grandparents left the Lithonia area where all their kin still resided, and came to Atlanta. My grandfather got a job as an Atlanta Police Officer. At the onset of the Depression, he was killed in a traffic accident while riding his police motorcycle. He left a widow and six children, the youngest being barely teenagers. My grandmother, Jane, had been orphaned at the age of eight and raised by relatives. She had married at sixteen and was now a single parent with no income. But she wasn't about to pull up stakes and return home because, for one thing, she really had no home to return to.

Although she lacked any training for office work she was an excellent seamstress and because she was the widow of a police officer, she was hired to work in the sewing room of Grady Memorial Hospital.

Henry W. Grady's last civic endeavor was working toward the establishment of a municipal hospital to serve the people of Atlanta and when it became a reality after his death, it was named for the *Constitution* editor. The hospital was known to those who worked there simply as Grady and anyone who heard the name knew the speaker was not talking about the monument. To many of the people who were born there, treated there, had babies there, and then died there, the hospital was known as "the Grady's" indicating that a site where so many things occurred had to be not just one place but many.

When Jane went to work at Grady all articles of clothing including uniforms for doctors and nurses, all uniforms for a rotating staff of interns and student nurses, all bed linens, and all the clothing worn by operating room personnel down to and including orderlies, was made by hand on the premises by the ladies who worked in the sewing room.

She was not long on the job when the woman in charge retired and Jane became head honcho of the sewing room. She supervised a staff of white women who numbered anywhere from six to eight because the turnover rate tended to be high due to the exacting demands of the job. If any employee couldn't carry her load, she had to be moved to some other job in the hospital or else let go. If the hospital ran out of an item you could not merely order a replacement from the store; the item had to be made by the ladies in the sewing room. This had been the policy since the incorporation of the hospital, and would remain the policy during Jane's long tenure.

But Jane was by no means confined to the hospital's basement sewing room. She was so fast that she could measure a new intern or nurse and run up a set of "whites" in no time flat. Her speed was legendary and during one harsh pneumonia and flu season, she and two other ladies turned out uniforms for an entire class of nurses in record time. When conditions were normal you could find her out on the receiving dock carefully inspecting the bolts of cloth which seemed to be delivered constantly to the hospital, or walking the corridors and inspecting hospital linens to be sure they were in mint condition and had been properly washed by the hospital laundry, or checking her doctors and nurses to be sure the clothes she had made for them made them look like the people they were supposed to be. In those days hospital staff did not wear name tags, for there was no need because you knew who you were and everybody else knew you were staff because of the way you were dressed.

Growing up, it was certainly convenient for me to have a grandmother with hospital clout. Being at Grady one morning to have a previously set broken arm checked out, I stopped by Jane's bailiwick to see what was going on. Believe you me, like always, there was commotion in the sewing room (another reason for the large turnover of personnel but Jane thrived on it) as people came and went as Jane conducted business, gave advice to hospital personnel, and dealt with all the crises of the day. As I arrived she was having a conference outside in the hallway with one of her sewing room ladies.

"I simply can't do it, I simply can't do it," the lady kept repeating to Jane. She seemed very distressed and agitated and I thought at first she was saying she was unable to keep the fast pace Jane insisted all her ladies maintain. And was she going to get the ax right now?

"Now, now, that's all right—just you settle yourself down. I understand, I understand," Jane told the lady as she patted her on the arm in an effort to smooth things over. "Now, just don't worry yourself about it anymore," Jane said very soothingly. "I know what a fine worker you are—I'll take care of it. You go ahead and start on the uniforms for the white nurses." The lady heaved an audible sigh of relief and literally ran back into the sewing room and got things going on her machine—double time.

After a quick but thorough inspection of my arm cast and wanting to know what the doctor said and who was the doctor, and without missing a beat, Jane and I walked back into the sewing room.

A tall thin black man with a quizzical look on his face was standing beside a great pile of cloth. Jane took her tape measure and began taking the man's measurements and talking at the same time wanting to know where he was from, who hired him and for what job? When he said that he had been hired as an orderly and was to begin the 2nd shift that afternoon, Jane, who by this time had finished measuring and was jotting the numbers down on a pad looked up with a start when the new employee told her he would be working the 2nd shift that day.

"Well! That will take some doing," she commented to herself. To him she said: "Now you get down here and pick up your uniform before you go on duty on the floor. You've got to have your uniform on before you go to work—do you understand?"

"Oh Yes M'am, yes M'am," the man replied as a broad grin came across his face, and with a sigh of relief he exited the sewing room.

Jane went in search of the superintendent of the hospital as she accompanied me out of the building. She wanted to know if I was certain which streetcar I needed to catch, and where to catch it, to take me back to school. Then she spoke about the incident in the sewing room. The lady was so upset because she could not take a black person's measurements because she had been brought up to believe that it was wrong for a white woman to be that intimate with a black man.

Grady was a hospital for both blacks and whites, but it was also a Segregated hospital. There were black wards for black patients who were treated by black nurses and black orderlies but there were no black doctors so white doctors treated black patients. There were separate wards for white people who were treated by white doctors and white nurses and also by black medical personnel if the need arose. The school of nursing was Segregated.

"It is not the same, not for most white ladies, they just can't handle it," Jane remarked as we walked along the busy corridor. Clearly, she was both amused but a bit exasperated by the lady's behavior, and although she understood it completely she obviously didn't think it was really the right attitude for the work place because it wasted time and in Jane's view there was no worse offense than that.

I did not realize it that day, but years afterward I would come to comprehend that Segregationist-minded white women like Jane were an evolving erosive influence upon Klan dominated thinking, and, would, nevertheless, be more inclined than white men to bend the rules of Segregation if common sense dictated that it was a more rational form of behavior.

ELEVEN

NOT SO DISTANT COUSINS

When he was sixteen, Ernest, the eldest son of Ellery and Almanza came to Atlanta and his uncle, Wideman Lee, got him a job at the livery stable. He lived with the Lee family in the West End and became familiar with that neighborhood and Atlanta. Next, he moved to northern Alabama where he was first an apprentice and later the straw boss of a sawmill. From there he moved on to south Georgia and operated his own sawmill along the Altamaha river. Then, he moved back to the Indian Fields and began cotton farming on the Lee Plantation.

The Lee home had burned but there was a log cabin still standing on the property where Wideman Lee's grandparents had first settled when they came to the Indian Fields. Ellery had recently acquired the property at auction simply by paying the back taxes.

Ernest and his young bride, Eva, (who were my maternal grandparents) had grown up on a farm that adjoined the eastern slope of Stone Mountain, moved into the cabin and set up housekeeping. The living conditions were pretty primitive, but the young couple thrived in the pre-boll weevil era because cotton prices were skyrocketing. Soon, they were living in a grand house on an adjoining plantation that Ellery had acquired. By the time they moved to the new place they already had two daughters and a third daughter was born there. The daughters were named Lila, Erna, and Marguerite. The girls were named by Ernest and had German names because they were named for women in the family of Almanza's maternal grandfather who had emigrated from Germany to fight in the American revolution. The fact that Eva had no say in the naming of her own daughters was not unusual in this time in the South. The father by custom had this prerogative and the mother wasn't usually consulted unless the father, as was many times the case, had no interest in the matter.

Ernest grew restless back in the Indian Fields, and just when cotton prices were booming he decided to pull up stakes and move his family to Atlanta. Ellery, who was at his peak as the most productive cotton grower in that part of the county, was flabbergasted. He could not understand why Ernest would abandon cotton when he could obviously get rich growing the white gold. But Almanza came to Ernest's defense. She always insisted her eldest son had been born with the Lee lust for adventure and needed to be moving on and exploring new ways of living.

At this point in time Ivy Lee was on the verge of becoming world famous, and Ernest, who was the same age as his cousin, no doubt felt like the world was passing him by, and he was determined to move to Atlanta and settle in the West End in the hope the location would do as much for him as it had for Ivy Lee.

Ernest got a job as a streetcar operator. Things were going smoothly, and he and Eva, who had already lost one young son to pneumonia, had another son whom Ernest named Ivy Lee Mason in honor of his famous cousin. Then things went bust.

Ernest was not cut out to be a streetcar man and when the streetcar he was operating crashed into a pie wagon at Five Points one block from the Grady monument, he quit the streetcar business that day.

Eva asserted herself. She loved city life. She loved living in the West End. She loved meeting new people and making friends. She was out of the country and well on her way to getting the country out of her.

Eva persuaded her husband not to go back to the country, but to remain in the city. Ernest was not all that eager to return to cotton farming. The onset of World War I had caused cotton prices to plummet drastically because of the British blockade of European cotton-importing seaports.

With several false starts of schemes that did not pan out, Ernest, nevertheless, finally got things going when he opened a restaurant along the streetcar line from the West End to downtown Atlanta. When America entered World War I and soldiers were stationed at a post just south of the West End, the restaurant thrived. When Ernest got into building houses needed due to the influx of people moving to Atlanta during wartime, Eva took charge of the restaurant and operated it at a profit. She was able to do this because the children were all in school and could help out at the restaurant after school hours.

No one raised in the country, and whose folks had been country gentry for several generations, ever took to the city with as much gusto as Eva. Those who would come to Atlanta from the farm because of economic necessity and would be unhappy and pine for the wide open spaces for the rest of their lives and would return to the country as soon as they could afford to, were not like Eva.

Eva, whose mother had taught school before her marriage, educated her daughter to have a life of the mind, and as a result, she loved books and read everything she could manage to get her hands on. She belonged to a women's club whose members worked for Women's Sufferage and other enlightened causes of the day. Eva was also an avid church goer and had read the Bible through many times. She enjoyed engaging the preacher in debate over liturgical interpretation of the Scriptures. When movies came to Atlanta, she became an avid movie goer and was glad the first two movie houses were located near the library so that she could check out books and see a movie all in one trip into town. Living in the city was, for Eva, living the good life.

The entire family came to think of themselves as city folks and when the Great Influenza Epidemic of 1918 hit Atlanta, and Ernest sold the restaurant and moved the entire family to Jessup in deep south Georgia for the duration, they were ready and eager to move back to the city as soon as possible.

Upon returning to Atlanta at the onset of the roaring twenties, Ernest returned to home building and Eva to all her clubbing and church activities. As the girls finished high school they all easily found office jobs (Margie was fired from her first office job when she defied her boss and had her shoulder length hair bobbed) for there was much demand for women who had office and clerical skills. They lived at the last stop on the streetcar line in the West End which had the dual advantage of being farther away from city congestion and the ready availability of public transportation.

But when Margie (one of Eva's first acts of self-assertiveness was to drop the then unusual and difficult name of her youngest daughter and call her "Margie" a name in a very popular song of the day) decided to get married she didn't choose one of the boys she had met in the city, but a man recently moved to Atlanta whose family roots had been in the Indian Fields for as long as her own. And this was not unusual. Newcomers to Atlanta would search for someone to marry who hailed from the same area where they grew up, and in this instance they were doing as their ancestors before them.

In fact, families of the Indian Fields were all related either by blood or marriage, and as a youngster in the company of adults I was often taken on a pilgrimage to various church cemeteries of the Indian Fields, and it was always a jolt to be told that the occupants of the same burial row were somehow related to both parents. In these times this too was ordinary and would remain so until World War II began the process of flinging people hither and yon.

When Margie married Herbert, who was Jane's eldest son, they settled in a house in the West End around the corner from Margie's parents. This too was the normal course of events.

When their first son was born he was named after his father and nicknamed Sonny, and four years later their second son was named by his father for his boss, and his middle name by his mother, for her doctor. Born thirty-nine days after Elvis, I would be a part of the generation which would bridge the gap that had always before separated the races in the South.

In the midst of the Great Depression and primarily because his father was one of the fallen, Herbert had become an officer with the Atlanta Police Department, and at the time I was born was the police aide and driver for Mayor James L. Key.

My namesake Mayor Key, was the first of a succession of Atlanta mayors who would lead Atlanta out of the political underbrush of Segregation and into the mainstream of modern American life.

Always outspoken and frank, Mayor Key had jumped into international fame while attending a conference of mayors in Paris, France.

"Prohibition is abominable," he stated to the press. "But the American people will change it one of these days. Seeing a country like France where there is no Prohibition, has convinced me that crime in American is due, in great part, to the 'dry' laws."

Upon his return to Atlanta Mayor Key faced a political uprising from a coalition of labor, church, and out-raged Prohibitionist groups. They secured the necessary petitions for a recall election and the Methodist bishop barred him from attending the Methodist church where he had taught the men's Sunday school class for many years.

Mayor Key began conducting his own Sunday services at a downtown Atlanta theater and taught a Sunday School class attended by 2,500 people. By the sheer force of his personality Mayor Key managed to rally the city to his side and win the recall election. The election was a rebuttal to the Prohibition forces in the capital of Southern Protestantism.

This election was a significant prelude for the city of Atlanta. It proved that Atlanta, under intelligent and vigorous political leadership, would in the future, and unlike other Southern cities, be open to the development of new ideas even to the point of rejecting by recall referendum, Prohibition, before the passage of its repeal had occurred anywhere else in the South.

During his time as aide to Mayor Key, Herbert learned much about Atlanta and became acquainted with city leaders because he and the mayor's secretary were the entire staff.

A meeting which occurred during the administration of Mayor Key concerning the employment of African-Americans into the all-white Atlanta Police Department has become a part of Atlanta folklore.

In the 1930s people who were not white, even if they could get registered, could only vote in national or general elections because Georgia along with the other states of the former confederacy had a White Primary law in the democratic(?) party, and since republicans in the South were virtually then non-existent, black people had no vote in city and state elections. Nevertheless, for the first time since the onset of Segregation, African-Americans were beginning to openly question the wrongness of Segregation. And in a city like Atlanta, with a major of Mayor Key's convictions, they could do so without fear of retaliation. In this time and in this place this was a great step forward.

At this historic meeting in the mayor's office was the publisher of the Atlanta *World*, a black newspaper, a prominent African-American Atlanta lawyer, and the Reverend Martin Luther King, Senior. They spent some time with the Mayor in urging the city of Atlanta to employ African-Americans as police officers.

There was no better way for African-Americans to attack Segregation than through the enforcement arm of the oppressor, for a Desegregated police force would toll the death knell of a Segregated society. But it would be a long time in coming.

The African-American delegation spent quite awhile discussing with the mayor the employment of black cops, and after they departed Mayor Key called his young aide into the office, and told him that such a thing was not possible for the present and would only be possible in the future when black people and white people had been educated to the idea. The mayor said that he had no doubt that such a thing would occur in the future and, turning around in his chair looked Herbert straight in the eye and told him it would one day be his responsibility to institute such a policy.

Still a young man in his late twenties when this obligation of sweeping social change first became a continuing part of his professional life, Herbert, over the next chaotic fifteen-year period which saw throughout the world the rise and ascendancy and fall of Fascism, never wavered in his determination to see that the Mandate imposed upon him by Mayor Key was abandoned.

Since I came into existence at the same time as the Mandate, I was always linked in Herbert's mind as a co-conspirator in the battle to bring an end to Segregation in the lives of the people of Atlanta.

The legendary meeting at city hall between Mayor Key and the African-American leadership of Atlanta marked the initial beginning of both races in the South uniting to end Segregation in America.

To me the irony of this classic encounter is the fact that both my namesake and my dad, on their mother's side, was a descendant of Cherokee Indians.

TWELVE

ALONG OLYMPIAN WAY SOUTH

Which of us has not remained forever prison-pent?
Thomas Wolfe: *Look Homeward, Angel!*

By the time I came to the West End the old neighborhood of Victorian grandeur had fallen victim to the ravages of passing time and was beset with peeling paint and a general aura of mildew. Clearly the West End was past its prime. She was like a woman no longer young who still put up a good front but when she came home at the end of the day and undressed it became apparent that she no longer bothered to shave under her arms.

That's not to say there wasn't life in the old girl still; she was just no longer number one. But her cultural legacy lingered on and my generation benefited mightily from the exposure.

Pundits are always saying nowadays that the present generation will be the very first generation of Americans who will not be better off than their parents. This is certainly not true in the South. Wars, repression by the North, economic panic and depression, a single product economy, and the boll weevil have made one generation of Southerners rich and the next generation poor. This seesaw effect has been the Southern norm rather than the exception.

In the West End the situation was of the general Southern pattern but also more personal; people began to value money above everything else. The priority of the West End had always been upon knowledge and learning and those who regarded this, and as a consequence all of the West End as being out-of-date, as soon as they could afford it, moved to the north side of town. But with the erratic nature of the Southern economy, this migration occurred over a period of several decades.

My early life in the West End was certainly rich. It was dominated by Eva who was the only person who was around everyday. When all the adults were at work, and Sonny was at school, the two of us filled our days with adventure.

When I was four years old I remember going to visit Lila, Eva's oldest daughter, who had recently moved to Morningside. Decked out in our Sunday best, we boarded the streetcar at the end of the line in the West End for our journey across town. Going into town, we passed through the busy commercial section of the city and rode the streetcar through a twisting tunnel that went under long lines of railroad tracks and emerged on Whitehall Street the busiest street in South Atlanta. In those days, all the many factory and wholesale houses were on Whitehall Street and the streetcar had to inch its way along because the street and sidewalks were always filled with automobiles and pedestrians. No matter the time of day or night, Whitehall Street was where the business of Atlanta was conducted.

Once we made it into downtown Atlanta, we had to transfer to another streetcar which we rode out Highland Avenue passed where the Carter Presidential Library is now located, on through Virginia-Highland, and out Highland Avenue to the very end of the streetcar line at Lanier Boulevard. The trip which took about two hours, was then from the very southwest city limits to the northeast city limits of Atlanta.

After getting off the streetcar, we had to walk two blocks to Lila's house. I was fascinated by a lawn sprinkler that was watering one of the lawns along the way for I had never seen one before. People in the West End did not water their lawns. The sprinkler was a big brass ring that shined brightly in the sunshine and sat in the middle of the yard and sprayed water upwards in such a manner that the lawn appeared to be covered by a massive, over-flowing crown. Yes indeed, the grass was certainly greener in Morningside than in the West End, a fact that even a four year old could grasp.

Lila's house though not new, had just been painted and smelled new. The back yard had just been landscaped and featured a small pond bursting with greenery and teeming with brightly colored goldfish. To Eva's immense chagrin, I immediately jumped into the pond and tried to grab one of the fish. A visiting neighbor lady suggested that perhaps I was merely hungry. A polite way of not saying the kid was from the south side of town, and, of course, what else could you expect?

During lunch, there was a terrific commotion on the street when the police arrived and amid much noise and blaring sirens carted the man of the house down the street off to jail. Seems that he had told everyone he made a living from investments but in fact was one of the most well-heeled bootleggers in the southeast.

On the way home, we stopped off at the library because Eva wanted to check out some books. She was never one to let anything interfere with her not keeping her reading library current. After a long wait we boarded the streetcar to the West End and I immediately fell asleep and did not awaken until we came to the end of the line. All the adults were home by this time and frantic about our whereabouts. Where on earth had we been? Hadn't we heard the news? Hitler had invaded Poland. Eva's only comment to this bombshell was to say that from all the racket on Lila's street that day, she thought for awhile that Hitler had invaded Morningside.

When I became old enough to walk the sidewalks of the West End on my way to school, I would pass by the once grand houses now converted either to apartments or rooming houses, or else inhabited by one sole remaining and aging member of a once energetic and on-the-go West End family. There was an old gentleman who when the weather was agreeable, played the violin every morning while seated in a rocking chair on the front porch, and as the children walked by he would serenade us grandly. A lady who wrote rather successful Gothic novels sat on the bench at the streetcar stop busily scribbling away in her Bluehorse notebook unaware of our presence or anything else, her mind far away as she plotted the perilous journey her characters would travel through the pages of her notebooks.

Once I could read and write I had to take Expression. Expression was very big in the South in those days. It was felt that children needed Expression to inspire self-confidence and build character.

Every Wednesday after school I would trudge up the hill on Olympian Way (many of the streets of the West End were named to evoke historical recollection) where a lady gave Expression classes. You had been assigned a poem or essay or oration to memorize at the previous class, and now having committed that passage to memory you had to stand up and recite it for the instructor. And not just once. You would have to recite the same passage several times until the reader was satisfied with your presentation. There were one-on-one hourly sessions with the instructor and the purpose was not simply to memorize and recite and forget, but to commit the passage to memory and repeat it with the proper voice range and inflection and to express yourself by what you were saying but also through what we call today body language.

These were individual sessions and you always had to wait in an adjoining room with the door closed while the kid ahead finished his or her session because the instructor took a lot of time with each student and was always behind schedule. You could hear the student ahead of you reciting as you tried to repeat your own assignment over and over to yourself so you could recite it properly. For me, Expression was a lifetime boon because in times of stress throughout my life, I would find myself repeating passages I learned then and manage to survive whatever crises then looming upon the horizon.

For all of my life, my dad had been in the Mayor's office but that came to an abrupt end about this time when one day he came home riding a police motorcycle rather than behind the wheel of the mayor's sleek Cadillac limousine. We were on the tip top and the next day out of office and at rock bottom.

This was the way I absorbed the news of the change in status, for the politics of the time I did not fully comprehend, but the significance of the motorcycle in the driveway instead of the long black limo, I grasped immediately. In politics, its the loss of the perks of office you always miss the most.

THIRTEEN

THE LIMBER TWIGS

Then, a big change occurred in the lives of Eva and Ernest. Although both Almanza and Ellery died long before I was born, their home in the Indian Fields had remained virtually empty. Ernest, with a Federal land bank loan backed by the Hoover administration had managed to save the Mason homeplace from being sold off the court house steps in the darkest days of the Depression. Countless other farms of the Indian Fields, and homesteads throughout the South and America, were unable to escape this fate.

The land bank loan was a program set-up to save farms from being foreclosed during the tough economic times of the early thirties. It was also designed to help President Hoover get re-elected but failed in that endeavor.

When the administration of President Franklin Roosevelt's agriculture department began alerting Southern farmers to the successful use of pesticides to control boll weevil damage to cotton crops, Ernest decided to move out of the West End and back to the Indian Fields and once again become a major cotton planter like his ancestors before him.

Eva was having no part of it. Her objection to moving to her mother-in-law's house was that it was dark and forboding, without modern conveniences, and, worst of all, in the country. Eva had become a city person and was determined to stay that way.

Throughout the early thirties Ernest went back and forth as he worked on modernizing the homeplace and preparing the long neglected cotton fields for cultivation.

During this time, Eva was concerned about the European situation. A Wilsonian democrat to the core, she was certain there would be a second world war begun in Europe and America

would be drawn into it, and her only son, Ivy Lee Mason, would
have to go off and fight. Therefore, these were tense times for
our family in the West End on the eve of World War II.

But it is most often not the things in life that we anticipate
which cause us so much heartbreak, but the intervention of the
totally unexpected.

Ivy Lee Mason, who had been married just a few weeks, entered the hospital to have a growth removed from his neck. It
was a minor routine surgical procedure and most of the family
was unaware it was going on. On the operating table his heart
stopped beating, and back then medical doctors had no knowledge of how to resuscitate a patient in such a situation, and the
patient died.

Ivy's death devastated his family. His three sisters adored
their only brother for many reasons, but mainly because as he
learned things growing up that then only male children were
privy to learn, he shared his knowledge with his sisters. When he
learned to drive an automobile, he immediately taught his sisters how to drive. This was radical behavior because the elder
generation did not think it proper for women to drive a car.

Neither Eva or Ernest ever really recovered from the death of
their only son, and although Eva would live another twelve
years, she only managed to do so because in her mind I was
available to take Ivy's place.

Overnight the pattern of my life changed radically. Summers
and weekends were now spent in the Indian Fields. It kept me
so busy I had to forsake Expression classes. This I regarded as a
definite plus. Ernest and Eva sold their home in the West End
and moved permanently to the Indian Fields. With Ivy's death
Eva abandoned her opposition to the plan and although she still
yearned for life in the city somehow that no longer mattered as
much as it had previously.

Ernest had managed to provide running water to the
homeplace by building a huge stone water tower and pumping
water by means of a hydraulic ram from a nearby spring. The
following year the Roosevelt administration through the REA
authority provided electric lights.

Big Susan, a black woman, who had come from the Indian
Fields and worked for Eva in the West End, but had soon departed because she didn't cotton to city living, was back in
charge of the kitchen in the country, and we were all glad to be
reunited.

I along with everyone else called the old homeplace "the country," and when leaving the West End to go there said "we are going to the country." The city was houses, businesses, sidewalks, paved streets, streetcars, buses, and automobiles. Everything else unpaved roads, cotton fields, barns, chicken houses, shade trees, and old homesteads—the country. There was no urban sprawl. The city, or towns, were one very distinct compact place and the rest was country. You were never confused about where you were.

I loved the country. I loved Eva and Ernest who I always called Mama and Papa. But the struggle to pay off the "Hoover" mortgage was never ending.

Everyday during the growing season Eva and Big Susan fed as many as eighteen "hands" everyday except Sunday and this was a big undertaking when everything had to be prepared everyday from scratch. Although the house had running water this was not drinkable; drinking water came from a well. When a rat or some other animal got into the well and drowned, the well had to be cleaned out. This was my chore, for I was the right size for the job. I had to be lowered into the well into the very bottom and bail-out any water still remaining.

Along with the usual farm chores it was my job in late Summer to bottle the sorghum syrup. The syrup was cooked from sugar cane in huge vats over fire in open pits and when it was "done" it was sent through a pipe to the syrup house which could be cut on and off like a water tap. Here it was made ready for the market by being bottled. There was always run-off from the tap and as I bottled the syrup I caught the run-off in a jar which I drank as the day wore on. By nightfall, I never wanted to even think about tasting sorghum syrup ever again.

It was also my task to gather eggs and pick fruit and vegetables. To be sure I did it right, Eva would sometimes accompany me. We were gathering Ellery's prized limber twig apples late one Summer afternoon and Eva insisted that the best fruit was in the very top of the tree. It always was.

I climbed up the tree and shook the apples loose and they cascaded downward. When I looked down I saw Eva lying motionless on the ground and I thought the apples had hit her on the head and killed her. I climbed down out of the tree and when I could not rouse her I ran and got Big Susan and we got a ladder and covered it with a blanket and made a litter and carried Eva back to the house. Ever afterwards, Eva had to take digitalis for the rest of her life.

When I had time off I walked across the road and visited with my cousins. They had a real tree house in a pear tree that was as big as a room in a house. The only other neighbors were the black folks who lived in the old Promised Land plantation and who still remembered about the time Margaret Mitchell came calling when doing research for *Gone With The Wind*.

Other times I would go rummaging through the old carriage house which was now a storage area. In it I came across Ellery's old desk and discovered all the papers and letters he and Almanza had kept over the years. I would read the papers and then discuss the contents with Eva. In the course of these discussions, it was decided that I should keep a journal which I began right off and kept working at, off and on, for the next two decades.

Eva may have forsaken the city for country life, but she did not abandon her keen interest in what was going on in the wider world. She subscribed to a variety of monthly magazines and ordered books from mail order catalogues. People would come to visit merely to borrow books to read. We soon were operating a regular lending library. Also, when old friends from the West End would drive out to visit they would take watermelons and peaches home with them and leave the latest books they had read in return.

We couldn't wait to read the new books. Eva would start off reading aloud and when she got tired, I would read aloud. If we liked a particular chapter, we would read it twice. In retrospect, it seems like I learned as much if not more, during the Summertime as I did during the school year.

Because I spent so much of my earliest years with individuals who were along in years, I thought this experience unique. When we are young we think that our first discovery is the very first discovery of all eternity. Only when we are older do we realize that along the way we have been journeying down an oft traveled road.

For Southerners the entire experience is more intense. I didn't grow up fast just because I was surrounded by older people. I was born old. All Southerners are born old. We are all at least 25 years old at birth. It is in our heritage, and the spirits of our ancestors travel down the chromosomes of our beings and never die. Southernness was passed on as though it was genetic. And the voices of our ancestors are forever clamoring to be heard.

From the front porch of the old homeplace you could see nothing but miles upon miles of white cotton bolls weaving in the wind; and in the distance the huge pile of granite, Stone Mountain, shaped like a silver-blue whale looming in an ocean of whirling white caps. In childhood it was both awesome and ordinary. It was just like the South.

Through me, I could feel my ancestors ricocheting down the generations yearning to be free. To be free of the legacy of rebellion and the oppression of racism.

In reality and in spite of the fact that she was a woman and not in the best of health and an in-law to boot, Eva bridged the gap between the aspirations of those family members who had preceded us—down to Herbert and me. With Herbert she was a constant ally and always an unwavering advocate for the end of Segregation. Herbert always said she was his closest friend and wisest supporter in this endeavor.

For me, the example was more direct. Along with all the other good folks who came to the homeplace, one afternoon a Klan recruiter, thinking I was a fulltime resident of the Indian Fields, approached me in the yard with the intention of getting me to work with a junior Klan group to keep white Americans from "having to go to school with Niggers."

I thought I had the discussion well in hand and was arguing diplomatically that the issue had not yet arisen, when Eva happened to look out the window to see who I was talking to. When she saw who the visitor was she knew immediately who he was and called for me to come into the house.

When I didn't respond immediately, she came out into the yard, and was holding two brooms made of bundled twigs and used for sweeping the yard. Southern country houses were surrounded by huge spreading oak trees to provide shade. Consequently no grass would grow under such thick cover and the red dirt following rainfall would turn to mud. To keep mud from being tracked into the house, Southern yards were covered with white creek sand and swept every Saturday.

Even though it was mid-week Eva handed me a broom and told me that we had no time for any conversation because "we had to sweep the trash out of the yard." When the intruder didn't take the hint and depart, Eva told him in no uncertain terms to scram. Not knowing exactly what else to do, and taken unawares, he did as he was told but in a very surly manner.

When Ernest got home, and I related to him what had hap-

pened, he cautioned me not to have any discussion with these
Klan people about anything and said that I should have gone
into the house immediately when Eva told me to. He said if
these people got it in for you, they would burn you out. He was
always telling Eva she should not speak out on the subject of
Segregation, and whereas he was as fair-minded as she, he
voiced a real concern for our safety.

All in all, I was sure that Eva relished her face to face confrontation with the enemy, and I swelled with pride secure in
the knowledge that what she had done that day was exactly the
right thing to do. At peace with the forces of the past inside my
being, I slept very soundly that Summer night.

FOURTEEN

THE AMEN CORNER

I cannot recall a time when I had not heard the tale about the blind mule that subsisted on sawdust. Like the struggle to end Segregation it had always been a part of my life. The myth of the South and the reality. The charm of the South and the backwater. The South of fable and of truth. This was my life and the life of everyone both black and white who lived in the South. The South was a region with a split personality. Southerners of every age and every color and every occupation were a people afflicted with schizophrenia.

Every afternoon I rode the streetcar from the West End to the police station in downtown Atlanta. It also was a journey from myth to reality.

By this time war was raging in Europe and the Pacific. With older members of the Atlanta Police Department dying off, and the younger members going off to war, there was an acute shortage of personnel, and Dad who was just beyond the draft age, moved up quickly in the police ranks because the immense effort generated by everyone toward ending the war caused Klan influence during these years to lessen. At this juncture in time, Herbert had been promoted and was captain of the Evening Watch.

Leaving the streetcar at Five Points I would walk the three blocks to the police station. This section of Decatur street had always been the most colorful in Atlanta, and in the era of Segregation it was the one place where the prevailing social laws were disregarded, not out of intent, but because this street since the founding of Atlanta had been the traditional street where the races intermingled. It was also the spot where the races began to divide and you could have only kept the races apart in this section by building a Berlin wall.

Since I soon became a regular along Decatur street I got acquainted with the inhabitants who operated businesses, resided, or simply hung out along the street. It was a truly Integrated bag.

There was the black movie theater, beauty parlor, barber shop, and clothing stores. Space was at a premium both on the street and sidewalk and in the stores. The barber shop occupied a large area and was therefore able to sell freshly-caught fried fish to go.

All the buildings had three floors and had been built in the last century by enterprising Atlantans who had operated businesses on the first floor and lived over the shop. By the time I came to Decatur Street those original developers had become wealthy and moved to Morningside. Some still came to town and operated businesses but most of the buildings had been leased by black people and newly arrived immigrants from Eastern Europe and the Middle East.

Every language and/or accent imaginable could be heard if not deciphered. Some of the second floor and nearly all of the third floor of the buildings had been converted to apartments and were occupied by African-Americans. The landlord was more than likely a newly arrived white person who spoke English with a heavy accent. Thus there was much waving of arms in the air and talking with hands and jabbing of fingers along the crowded sidewalks of Decatur street, but everybody got along. To hear a Jewish person born in the Ukraine speaking English with a Russian accent in a Southern drawl are sounds once heard that are never forgotten.

For me, Decatur street was tv before television was invented and a better show than the movies. This area of Atlanta was the heart of the city.

When I first started hanging out at the police station and along Decatur street an officer on the beat was my guide. Through him I got to know everybody and everyone got to know me. The folks were all very friendly and called me "Little Cap."

It was an intriguing world to a kid and in stark contrast to the West End and the Indian Fields—the places I had always known.

There was a lot more sex going on for one thing. This was a

neighborhood of adults and a very nice lady who operated a variety store was one of several establishments that was a legitimate business up front and a whore house in the back. This particular operation consisted of three back rooms one of which was known as the "Parson's" room where for a price a gentleman could spend some time with a lady of his choice. The Parson's room was equipped with a buzzer that could be set-off up front and a trap door whereby the occupant could exit out the back should a police raid occur. This almost never happened because the operators of these establishments knew everything going on in the neighborhood and were police informants. Only if they got involved big time selling moonshine whiskey or running the bug (an illegal lotto game where you waged daily bets on certain numbers) did the police come down on these people.

All the Madams were African-American as were the women. The clientele were black men and white men who wore suits. This was, after all, uptown.

When otherwise not engaged, the love ladies as they were most often referred to, hung out on Decatur Street. The love ladies all had shiny, close-cropped hair and dressed like Josephine Baker. Anywhere else in Atlanta, the love ladies would have been a scandal, but along Decatur Street no one cared. The lady who had the store with the Parson's room and I became great friends. Whenever I dropped by for a visit or to purchase notebook paper she insisted on letting me have a gum ball from the penny machine—at no charge.

Some other African-American women I came to know who lived together on Decatur Street almost directly across the street from the police station were quite different from the love ladies—they were a group of lesbians. These women managed to maintain a high status in a Segregated society because they didn't work as maids or cleaning women for white folks but had jobs in business concerns and factories then located in the downtown area. It both amazed and exhilarated me to know persons who traditionally had been on the very bottom rung of the ladder but had successfully vertically assaulted Segregation and thrived.

As I churned along the downtown sidewalks in the world of the time I felt that I had escaped from the confines of the black and white TV box and catapulted my being well into the next century. I thought I was living in Futureworld.

I would get to the police station in the afternoon and hang

around the general office where people in trouble with the law came and went. The old building had been built in the 1890s and had huge ceilings and massive rooms that echoed the never ending foot traffic.

A staircase led to the second floor where all the court rooms were located and since the jail was right behind the courtrooms, prisoners could be brought directly to trial without going out-of-doors and right into court without entering from the front which was always jammed packed with people when court was in session.

When the two officers who worked the main office were otherwise engaged I would cover the phones. My sole function was to inform whoever was calling to hold on until an officer was free to talk with them. Of course I considered this effort on my part vital to the functioning of the department and aiding the war effort. At an early age I had become involved in the inner workings of the city of Atlanta.

Dad and I were walking up Decatur Street toward town at a fast clip and I had to really hustle to keep up. Offices were emptying out for the day and the already over-crowded sidewalks became even more congested.

It was a particularly windy Winter afternoon when even more people than usual were scurrying about, when we came upon this big automobile parked in front of the old Trust Company of Georgia Building. A black chauffeur was standing by the car on duty and as we approached he greeted Dad warmly. My Dad seemed to know everybody: White and black, rich and poor, office workers and shoppers, outstanding citizens and those in trouble with the police. As we walked the streets of Atlanta he seemed to be greeting everybody we passed by and exchanged words of conversation without slowing down, for Dad was always in motion. But on this occasion we halted for a longer chat.

While Dad was talking to the chauffeur, I noticed two gentlemen coming through the crowd of people and were approaching the car and as they moved forward people in their path seemed to just melt away and give them room. It was kind of like watching the parting of the Red Sea.

As the much older of the two gentlemen approached the car he began hollering—

"Herbert!! Herbert!!" In an aged and screeching voice. In a flash, Dad was around the front of the car, and greeted the old gentleman, who carried a cane and was highly feeble and greatly agitated.

"Herbert, Herbert, you've got to do something about all this traffic!! Where in the blazes are all these people coming from?" He raised his cane and swirled it in the air and would have toppled over had not his chauffeur by this time reached his side and steadied him. When he did so the old man pulled away from him.

"I'm all right." He insisted.

At this point, the other man, who was about Dad's age or older, shook hands with him and then with me in a most formal yet cordial manner that I was totally unaccustomed of receiving from adults. Needless to say I was quite impressed.

While the elder gentleman talked with Dad the other man eyed me curiously and, I thought, with amusement. This made me very uneasy.

When the two gentlemen had approached the car and Dad realized their presence, he had been at their side at once, with me right behind him. Like I said before, when Dad decided to move, he did so quickly and if you were going to keep up with what was going on you had to do likewise. I prided myself on the fact that with much practice, I managed to keep up; so, on this occasion when Dad moved around the automobile and onto the sidewalk I was right behind him, and the chauffeur was standing in our wake; who, as I said, recovered quickly, and was now opening the rear door and attempting to help the elderly gentleman into the backseat who kept protesting that he didn't need all this fuss.

"What I need, Herbert, is for you to do something about all this traffic around my building so I can get in and out!!"

Dad assured him that he would certainly do something about all the traffic! As the car moved off into the traffic the other man had a brief conversation with Dad and then turned to re-enter the bank building. Then he stopped and turned toward me:

"You certainly know how to move swiftly, young man." And very quickly was gone.

As we walked on toward the restaurant, Dad was giving me a rundown on the people I had just met. He was like a computer with a storehouse of information in his head about Atlantans.

"The old man—that was Ernest Woodruff. He doesn't get downtown too much anymore. I guess that is why he was surprised at the traffic. There must have been a board meeting of the bank . . . the other man was Bob Woodruff, his son. When

Ernest Woodruff bought the Coca-Cola Company from the Candler family his son Bob became president."

I immediately thought of all the wall clocks and lunch trays and school-crossing safety signs provided for my school and was impressed to have met the man who provided them.

Many years later, I was always chagrined that at the time I had little comprehension of the magnitude of the chance sidewalk encounter.

Robert Woodruff would make Coca-Cola known all over the planet. He would use the profits from Coca-Cola in such a manner, for the betterment of the people of Atlanta, that even Warren Candler would have been stunned. And, he would support Mayor Hartsfield unflinchingly to end Segregation in America.

The streets of downtown Atlanta became my education. The extraordinary mix of people and races and social classes all moving about together on the same thoroughfares influenced my thinking for the rest of my life.

When things were quiet along Decatur Street, I would go over to Grady Hospital and see Jane. Things were always popping there. Although never called pretty, Jane was often described as being a "very handsome lady." With her regal manner, imperial carriage, high cheekbones, and piercing Indian eyes inherited from her Native American ancestors, even more than Herbert, she could stare down anyone who was not keeping up with the program.

One day I went with her to put Patsy on a bus to Jacksonville, Florida. Patsy was an African-American woman who had worked for Jane all her life. The saying was: Where Jane goes Patsy is sure to follow.

Patsy was traveling to Florida to attend her grandmother's funeral. Patsy had never traveled anywhere that far alone and had much trepidation about making the trip. Sensing Patsy's uneasiness, Jane immediately took charge of everything and got me to go along to the bus station with them so Patsy would not feel so alone.

I could not have been more wrong thinking I was simply part of a send-off party. First off, the bus driver tried to load Patsy's bag in the luggage compartment, and Jane insisted that instead Patsy take it aboard the bus with her, for it not only contained clothes but food that Jane had prepared and a flashlight because it would be dark soon. Why Jane thought Patsy would have need of a flashlight traveling on an interstate bus, I could not fathom.

Next, Patsy did not board the bus alone, we all did because Jane was determined to find Patsy a proper place to sit even though by law it had to be next to a black person and in the rear of the bus. When she found a teenage girl seated next to an obviously elderly drunken man, she insisted that the bus driver move the man elsewhere so the two women could sit together.

"I'm certainly not going to have Patsy seated next to an old drunk on this long trip," Jane stated firmly to both no one and everyone.

With the two women seated Jane and I continued to occupy the center aisle of the bus as we all engaged in conversation.

Finally, in exasperation, the bus driver exploded. "Lady, are you finished? Will you please get off my bus!! I have a schedule to keep!!!"

Patsy spoke often about her trip to her grandmother's funeral recounting all the events of that important journey in her life. At the end of her recitation she would repeat with emphasis what her seatmate said to her on the bus trip to Jacksonville.

"Who in the world was that bossy white lady? And why did she make Daddy go and sit in the back of the bus?" Jane stories of this nature were legion.

To complete the family triangle in government offices, I would stop off at the state capitol and visit my Aunt Erna.

The 1920s in Atlanta were boom times. There was not only an increase in business activity but growth in home and commercial development. Office buildings, taller than any previously built, began rising in the downtown area. City government was hiring people in the expanded health, police, and fire departments.

People were going to work at the state capitol in newly created state jobs. Atlanta had progressive city government that built the first major airport in the Southeast. The whirlwind that would eventually propel Atlanta into national and international prominence was in its infancy.

I used to look at a photograph of Erna and my mother, as they had been photographed as they were going to lunch from their earliest jobs. I know from my mother's short hair that it had to have been taken in the early to mid-twenties.

The two young women in the photograph were dressed in short skirts and jackets tailored for office wear. My mother was wearing a white shirt and dark tie tied in a man's knot. The photograph could just as easily been taken now as then.

Out of college and into the job market of Atlanta in the twenties, Erna landed a job at the state capitol. Of Eva's three daughters, Erna was the only one to graduate from college. Although she had earned a degree in journalism, she took the job with the state because the state offered her a more varied career and a chance to really do something in the world. She was among the first college educated, career-oriented women to be hired by state government.

Erna joined the fledgling State Health Department almost at the time of its inception. There was a push on to get government involved in the lives of the people other than when they went to the post office to purchase a three cent stamp. The birth of the welfare state was upon us. We decry this development nowadays without fully comprehending how bleak our world would be today without it.

The terrible plagues upon the people in those days were then manifold but now largely forgotten because government took steps to combat them.

The State Health Department's number one priority then was the eradication of rabies. Individuals bitten by mad dogs had to endure countless numbers of sera injections. One was warned to be always on the look out for mad dogs, of dogs which seemed to be deranged, or foamed at the mouth. Children were told to run in the house, climb a tree, or flee into the barn to escape being bitten by a rabid dog. It was the scourge of the day.

Erna had an office in the basement of the capitol building. We would visit her there and she would wax eloquent on the subject of rabies eradication as she conducted visitors through the state laboratories where eager young, white-coated employees were at work.

If an individual was bitten by a strange dog, and if it was not known whether or not the dog was rabid, the animal's head was severed from its body, and the head shipped to the state lab for analysis. If the dog was not rabid then the person would be spared the anti-rabies injections, a procedure which heretofore had been mandatory because most dogs were not then given shots and there was no way of knowing if an animal was rabid unless it exhibited outward signs. I went home and held my pet dog protectively. Visions of her guillotined head ending up in the bowels of the state capitol sent shudders through my body.

The other plague of the day was ringworm. The eradication of ringworm in children of the South was the number one priority of the region's health services. It was like today's drug problem. Not only government money but private money was expended to eradicate ringworm.

The State Health Department received a grant from the Rockefeller Foundation to fight ringworm. Erna drove all over the state lecturing to hospital personnel, schools, and churches teaching people about the problem. We all listened wide-eyed as she described the particular backwardness in some areas of the state, and heard her speak in dismay at how much distrust there was among some people to participate in state programs. It was a mammoth undertaking.

Later Erna's department moved out of the basement of the capitol and into grand new quarters in a magnificent building across the street. We had all trooped into town to inspect the new building. It was awesome. Massive bronzed doors, Georgia marble floors, and huge new offices. It was like a palace, I thought.

As the years went by Erna began to see change occurring and she told us joyously of how progress was taking hold and that the lives of the people were better. To her great satisfaction and credit she saw in her time the complete eradication of ringworm in Southern life. It had been a joint endeavor of advances in medical treatment and educating the people to the problem. She could take immense pride in the role she played in the latter effort.

Her travels about the state earlier on in her career convinced Erna that there had to be a better way for the Health Department to disseminate information to the public. Changes in health procedure were occurring almost daily and people needed to know what was going on.

The Health Department allowed Erna to create and edit a monthly magazine on good health practices and changes in medical science. It was the beginning of our present day awareness of what is good for you healthwise and what is bad.

Georgia's Health began as a small circulation, free health magazine which went mostly to hospital workers, schools, and community groups throughout the state. By the early sixties it was the most read of state publications.

But by then we had all become so health aware that newspapers, radio, and television was telling us hourly what was bad for us and what was good. Again, we all took great pride in Erna's pioneering effort in this aspect of making life better in the

South.

During World War II, Erna had to take on extra responsibilities as the men went off to war. Not satisfied that her job was sufficient labor on behalf of the war effort, she underwent nurse's aid training and did volunteer nursing in an Atlanta hospital throughout the war.

From Fanny Kemble to Lillian Carter, women in the South have been in the vanguard of the attack on the moral wrongness of first slavery and then Segregation. Erna was always quick to point out that the State Health Department was the only body of state government to disregard Segregation when providing services to Georgians. More than that, she practiced what she preached.

In the Christmas season of 1943, Erna came to our house in the West End for dinner. Afterwards, Erna drove Mother, and Sonny, and me over to Spelman College to hear that renowned women's chorus and accompanying men's choir from Morehouse College present their celebrated program of Christmas music.

We parked the car and trooped into the building. The hall was full but we managed to find seats in the balcony. We were the only white people seated in the balcony. We were seated next to black people. When the races in the South mingled it was standing up. Any integrated seating in the South in a public place was illegal. We were breaking the law, but nobody came and arrested us. The world had not gone up in flames.

It was no great insight on my part to comprehend that this was an historic event of broader impact beyond the way it affected me. For even a dullard would have noted that in a Segregated world this was a rigorously Non-segregated occasion. Children are influenced by positive words on morality, much more so by events.

No other happening in my life made more clear to me why Segregation was evil. From that night onward, what had always been implanted in my being from my past, had now become my conscious determined policy.

Across Washington Street from the state capitol was a Baptist Church, Presbyterian Church, Catholic Church, and one block away an Episcopal Church and Trinity Methodist Church. All the influential denominations in Atlanta were situated on the corner of Washington and Mitchell Streets. Across Mitchell Street was the city hall and a block to the west, the court house.

The corner of Washington and Mitchell Streets was referred

to as the Amen Corner. It was so called because of all the churches clustered around the corner, but also because the capitol and city hall were both on this corner and with so many politicians always gathering in this area it was thought that the only hope for ordinary citizens was a few words of prayer.

In the years ahead, the Amen Corner would become the focal point of civil discontent. Barely a year after the close of World War II, the very first protest march in the South by Atlantans demanding the employment of black policemen developed when about two-hundred African-Americans marched from Auburn Avenue, the heart of the black business district, south onto Washington Street carrying signs and posters.

The marchers did not disrupt automobile traffic. The march was orderly. It proceded passed the state capitol and turned at the Amen Corner, stopped briefly on the steps of city hall, and then back to Auburn Avenue without interference or confrontation with the police or anyone else.

State workers and employees of the city of Atlanta out on the street returning from their lunch break, didn't really comprehend what the march was all about and thought it was a civic or church group promoting some African-American function. Even if they actually read the signs some of the marchers were holding aloft, the message did not sink in. The idea of employing African-Americans as real Atlanta policemen was an idea so beyond the comprehension of the ordinary white Atlantan that he or she simply could not fathom what this great-granddaddy of civil rights marches was all about.

In those days Southerners thought the term civil rights had to do with the American Revolution, and nothing to do with anything on the streets of Atlanta, Georgia.

But the die was cast. Feeble as this first march appears today, it signalled the beginning of the end of Segregation in America.

FIFTEEN

MAGNOLIA GRANDIFLORA

Among the magnitude of things handed down to us from the Greeks is the tradition of strong urban generals.

Pericles was the greatest general, or mayor, of Athens. He dominated the city council, built new buildings, and expanded the Democratic process. The influence of his political aura spread from the Agora of Athens to all future cities where Democracy prevailed.

The Periclean Age in Athens occurred in 500 B.C. The Hartsfield Era took place in Atlanta over two millennia afterwards.

The time from Athens to Atlanta covered centuries; the form of government as exercised by Pericles and echoed by Hartsfield was that of brothers.

Then, the influence of Hartsfield's time in Atlanta in the latter decades of this century traveled to city halls and court houses all over Dixie.

Historically Mayor Hartsfield became the defacto Big Daddy of a rising generation of New South political leaders because he was the first elected official in Dixie who proposed and practiced an enlightened racial policy. He supported the emergence of African-Americans upon the political scene and laid the groundwork for the end of Segregation in the South. Until the Hartsfield era in Atlanta, no man could be influential in the South if he challenged the rigid system of legal Segregation. Hartsfield did so and got away with it. The South has never been the same since.

Although the South suffered from shortages and inflation in the years following World War II, economically the region was booming and for the first time in generations was really beginning to come out from under the poverty of Reconstruction,

Sharecropping, and Depression.

But both blacks and whites wanted a part of the action in the after-war South. First the New Deal and then massive Federal spending in the South on war production, had opened to brown eyes and blue eyes alike not only the hope but the expectation of a better life.

The traditional white Southerner was determined to maintain Segregation at all costs. Black people were determined to bring about changes but were stiffled by the system of Segregation which had ruled both legally and informally in the South for a hundred years.

A wedge was forced into the otherwise solid wall of legal Segregation by the Federal courts. In 1945 the Supreme Court outlawed the Democratic White Primary. This decision was followed in 1954 with the outlawing of Segregation in public schools. The Segregationist wall was cracked but white Southerners moved swiftly to stiffle the breach with a policy of *massive resistance*. But the opening in the wall made blacks more determined than ever. They became militant in response to *massive resistance* and the line between the opposing groups was clearly drawn.

Southern whites, always partial to guns as the backbone of their national heritage, began arming themselves at an appalling rate. While black leaders consistently opposed violence and implored black people not to resort to arms, sales of guns to blacks acclerated as racial tension increased. The South rapidly became an armed society. Guerrilla warfare between two racial groups seemed possible as the region tottered precariously atop a mountain of armaments.

The factor which contributed most to a change in the Southern climate was the fact that the city of Atlanta moved aggressively to abort violence and abandon years of black oppression. This progressive outbreak in Atlanta was no doubt favored by the conditions of the time, but it was due mostly to the presence in the mayor's office of an extraordinary American politician.

William Berry Hartsfield was born in Atlanta on March 1, 1890, about five blocks from Five Points, the hub of downtown Atlanta. He was the last mayor of Atlanta to grow up, near the railroad tracks, in the heart of 19th century Atlanta. His father had come to Atlanta soon after Sherman's departure and set-up a tinsmith's shop just as the ashes from the holocaust cooled. As a child Hartsfield's mother often told him of watching Sher-

man's exit from Atlanta and of the looting and destruction
which followed. The total destruction of Atlanta as a result of
the Civil War, a war that came about because of the presence in
the South of two different races, was something that was vividly
alive to Hartsfield all his life.

As mayor of Atlanta in the years when racial unrest accelerated, the horror of Atlanta being destroyed once as a result of
racial strife was much on his mind, and he was determined that
such a thing would not happen again if he could help it.

Hartsfield was sixteen years old when the then worst race riot
in the history of the United States exploded in Atlanta. The riot
lasted for three days as roving bands of white men indiscrimi-
nately attacked blacks. When it was all over ten blacks and two
whites were dead and 170 people injured. It made a lasting im-
pression on Hartsfield.

In that hot August of 1906, there had been a four-man race for
governor of Georgia. One candidate, taking Southern demagogu-
ery to new heights, proposed that blacks be barred by law from
voting in general elections. The proposal solidified Segregationist support and swept this candidate into the governor's office.
He carried the rural areas of the state and the city of Atlanta as
well.

But the racial animosity stirred-up by this campaign provoked
the race riot. Hartsfield had supported one of the losing candidates—this election being his first venture into politics. He was
astounded at the direction the election took, and stunned by the
resulting riot. It was etched in his memory forever that Southern
politicians, in their greed for political office, could create such
awful havoc by fanning the flames of the racial issue.

As a young man in Atlanta Hartsfield attended business
school. He loved the city and wanted to make a career for himself. It never occurred to him to go anywhere else. Pretty quick
he was a law clerk with one of the city's big legal firms. He enjoyed the law but felt that just reading law restricted his education. He had never traveled and felt that he did not know what
was going on outside Atlanta and the South. He wrote to the
Dean of a dozen colleges for book lits and went through Doctor
Eliot's Five Foot Shelf. His special favorites were writers like
Thackery and Dickens whose works highlighted the need for social reform and civic progress.

In 1921 Hartsfield opened his own law office in Atlanta and
entered politics. He was elected to the City Council and was one

of the first to call for an investigation of the graft and corruption that was then a way of life around City Hall.

Of all Hartsfield's forward-looking endeavors later in his career, his early grasp of the effect of air travel upon society in the future (he learned to fly himself) was as farsighted in civilian affairs as Billy Mitchell's was in military matters. As Chairman of the Aviation Committee of City Council, he persuaded the city to purchase a race track on the outskirts of town for the use of a city airport. This formed the nucleus of what is today Hartsfield International Airport.

Chafing in the ward-heeling atmosphere of City Hall, Hartsfield ran, and was elected to the state legislature. But the Georgia legislature was dominated by rural forces, and Hartsfield quickly realized that he was a lone urban man in a rural world and had no chance for advancement in state politics.

It was often said by people in politics, many of whom were Hartsfield's bitterest political foes, that had he been from any other section of the state but Atlanta, Hartsfield would have easily been elected governor because of his ability and superb campaign techniques and oratorical style.

The fact that Hartsfield was discriminated against in state politics because he was from Atlanta really burned him up. As a young politician he buried his resentment and preceded with a career in Atlanta politics but later in his life when racial unrest arose and a conflict of what was good for Atlanta and what was good for the state appeared to be at odds—at least in the thinking of state politicians—this old resentment against the state welled up inside him and made him determined to see Atlanta safely through the Desegregation crisis.

Atlanta has never experienced anything before or since like the first Hartsfield Administration. In his inaugural address, Hartsfield pledged to the citizens of Atlanta that he would work tirelessly to make Atlanta a great city. Most of those in his audience were wary because anything different meant change, and all those who had a hammerlock on city government wished for things to remain the same. A contingent of Klan leaders arrived at city hall early and took front row seats in the council chamber as the mayor began his address. They did not trust this new young mayor and wanted him to know that he had better not mess around with them. All things considered, one wonders why anyone would have wanted the job of mayor of Atlanta.

The city was $3,000,000 in debt and bankrupt. The new

mayor's first priority was to get the city's finances in order. He pledged economy and efficiency in government and maintained this policy for a quarter of a century. He made repeated trips to New York to plead with the money lenders to raise the city's financial rating so that bond money for much needed city improvements could be secured at the lowest rate of interest possible. He succeeded in getting the city of Atlanta's rating upgraded from the lowest to the highest rating—an incredible feat for a Southern mayor in those years.

Hartsfield's second priority was to restore integrity and faith of people in government. The old political cronies on the City Hall scene had never seen anything like it. Previously a new mayor employed his friends or those who had supported him in his election and the mob usually descended upon City Hall en masse seeking jobs. Hartsfield would have none of this. He went out and sought the best people he could find for city jobs. He was undaunted by entrenched opposition and breezed onward.

The mayor was full of bounce, had piercing blue eyes, and was so thin that he appeared taller than his just under six feet height. He had a wife grin that appeared too big for his face which he flashed at political friends and foes alike.

Hartsfield was in sharp contrast to the pot-bellied, cigar-chomping, tobacco-spitting pols who populated the City Hall scene. He smoked cigarettes but soon discovered when he became mayor that he was constantly fatigued and went to the doctor to find out what was wrong. It never occurred to him that since becoming mayor he literally had not stopped working at the city's business seven days a week. The doctor told Hartsfield that he was fatigued because of smoking and that if he would quit he would have more energy. Hartsfield quit smoking that very day. He well knew that the task he had set for himself required all the energy he could muster.

Having started a clean-up of city government, Hartsfield was determined to clean-up the city. Atlanta had come into existence with the railroads. All those coal-burning engines pulling trains in and out of Atlanta. They never stopped running for they were the life blood of the city. But this made downtown Atlanta one of the dirtiest cities in America.

Hartsfield demanded to know why the railroads could not stop sending all those smoke-belching steam engines through town, and although it was a long battle, by the mid-forties he succeeded in keeping all the steam engines out of the city, as the railroads began converting to diesels. Once he got the steam engines out of town, he launched a public and private clean-up of city buildings. For the first time, with the soot and grime washed away, Atlantans could tell what their churches and other buildings looked like. I will never forget the first time I passed by the Amen Corner and saw the churches cleaned down to their glistening Arabia Mountain granite.

Hartsfield was resolved to have a downtown city park and a fountain. A city without a fountain was a hick place. In his travels, he noted how much prettier other cities looked to the visitor with their tree shaded parks, landscaping, and fountains. Atlanta had none of this downtown. It had to build too fast too many times to pay much attention to this kind of civic improvement. Individual Atlanta neighborhoods were rightly famous for their elegance and had more trees than other places, but the central city was grim and dirty since Atlanta had never been planned and had grown-up along the railroad tracks.

The area in front of the city auditorium was an abandoned coal yard and eyesore much in need of civic beautification. Hartsfield decided to have a park there, and in spite of the opposition of the nay-sayers, succeeded in doing so. Of course the central feature, and main attraction of this first of several other downtown parks to come, was a fountain. It was equal in size and grandeur to any civic fountain anywhere. At nightfall, Hizzoner herded groups of civic enthusiasts to the park as the fountain with the aid of spotlights, became a dazzling outdoor display of fantasy, color, and light. All who saw it swelled with pride in Atlanta and its beauty.

It soon became the big thing to do on Summer nights to go downtown and watch the dancing waters of the fountain and oooooooooohhhhh and aaaaaaaaaaahhhhhh over its cascading rainbow of colors.

I thought the fountain was just the greatest thing ever and could not get enough of viewing the changing of the colors. It was like fireworks exploding out of water. For a five-year-old in the era before television, it was pure magic.

All at once, my dad was pulling on my arm, shaking me and trying to get my attention because the fountain held me in a trance. My dad was talking to this man, and pointing toward me and this man came over to me and bent down and put his smiling face right into my face and wanted to know what I thought of the fountain.

"I think it is mi-ra-cu-lous!!" I intoned in a deep Southern drawl which seemed to be coming from elsewhere.

My excitement over the fountain caused the smiling man and another man and woman who were with him, to roar with laughter. Of course I thought they were laughing at me and I looked away from them and down at my feet. The lady quickly rushed over to me and bent down, and opened her purse and offered me chewing gum. This caused me to brighten considerably. I began talking about the fountain once again for there was no shutting me up on the subject, and at this time in my life I talked of little else. Again, I insisted it was miraculous. I had picked up the word from Bible school and thought if it was good enough for the church it was good enough for the fountain.

For years afterward, when I encountered Margaret Mitchell, she would re-tell to whomever was present, the story of our first meeting.

With Margaret Mitchell that evening had been her husband, John R. Marsh, to whom she had dedicated *Gone With The Wind*. I had the hardest time trying to comprehend how Margaret Mitchell could be married to Mr. Marsh. In the West End, if two people were married they always had the same last name. As a consequence, in the years ahead, and to her immense delight, whenever I encountered the author of *Gone With The Wind*, I always addressed her as Mrs. Marsh.

But it was the chance encounter with Mayor Hartsfield which would most affect me. Over the next twenty years we developed a remarkable friendship which survived the era of accelerating social change and endless discussion and periodic shouting matches over what was the best course to follow for the betterment of all of the people of the city of Atlanta.

I cannot stress too strongly the effect the fountain and the park had upon us because the fountain, in those long Summers prior to the war, brought people together. The park was like a town square where people gathered in the evening to visit and discuss the events of the day.

Dad met people and discussed city affairs with those whom he had not seen much of since his days at city hall, and more importantly, it provided the opportunity for he and Mayor Hartsfield to mend their political fences.

As a result, my dad became Mayor Hartsfield's most fervent supporter within the Atlanta Police Department. This new alliance was in the best interest of both men, and, as it turned out, in the very best interest of the city of Atlanta. It was often said by political observers of the day that Atlanta would never have made it out of the shadows of the past with just one of these individuals; it had to have both.

Eugene Mitchell, Margaret Mitchell's father, had been a long-time supporter of Mayor Key and Peggy, as she was known before she was famous, and my dad had known one another for years. Many years later, Mayor Hartsfield told my mother that it was Margaret Mitchell's constant championing of my dad that helped convince him that he should patch things up politically with Mayor Key's one-time aide.

Mayor Hartsfield wanted not only to have a fountain in the park, but tree-shaded walks flanked by giant magnolia trees that would give the right backdrop to the mighty fountain. Again, there was a mighty chorus saying it couldn't be done, but Hartsfield, undeterred, began cruising the city's residential neighborhoods seeking the finest specimens to be found of *Magnolia Grandiflora*. When Hizzoner found the trees he wanted people said that such big trees could not be successfully transplanted. But Hartsfield didn't give up. He was determined to move the trees to the new city park where homefolks and visitors alike could enjoy their beauty. The South was famous for its magnolias. People coming to Atlanta expected to see them, and, by God, they had a right to see them!! It was Southern good manners. Anybody who was against that was against Atlanta. The big-tree owners sold their cherished *Magnolia Grandiflora* to the city and under Hizzoner's personal supervision they were transplanted in the new city park.

From this episode Hartsfield learned that by appealing to the ordinary citizen's sense of pride, he could prevail and have his way and promote whatever program he was pushing.

But it was as master of ceremonies at the week-long festivities celebrating the world premiere of the movie *Gone With The Wind* that the first Hartsfield Administration reached its glorious climax. The mayor realized at once the publicity value Atlanta could garner from the movie version of Margaret Mitchell's famous book.

The premiere week in December, 1939, the mayor was in constant motion. The city was jammed with movie stars, visiting dignitaries, and newspaper people. This was the first chance for Hartsfield to get to know the national press and for the national press to get to know him. He provided press room space at City

Hall, lined-up press tours of the city, and held a press conference about every half-hour. If he was not racing to the airport to greet another star or visiting celebrity, he was arranging details of the opening night show.

At Hartsfield's urging, the facade of the movie theater where the premiere was to be held was converted to look like the *Tara* plantation in the movie. In front of the columns, and standing beneath a picture of Scarlett O'Hara and Rhett Butler, Hartsfield welcomed the dignitaries to the first showing of the movie. All the stars were there: Clark Gable and his wife Carole Lombard, Vivien Leigh and her husband-to-be, Laurence Olivier, Olivia de Havilland, David O'Selznick, and Mr. and Mrs. John Marsh. Hartsfield took charge of the ceremonies and traded quips with everyone who entered the theater. He performed so well and handled the proceedings with such showmanship that the stars and moguls of Hollywood were quite impressed. A lasting friendship grew up between the cast and the mayor of Atlanta.

Hartsfield was a master at getting press coverage whether at home or abroad. In a time when most Southern politicians thought public relations was something dirty, Hartsfield had mastered the art. With animals he positively outdid himself.

When Roy Rogers came to town with his horse Trigger, it was a natural. The mayor had them both in his second floor City Hall office for a press conference and picture-taking session. In the midst of the general mayhem Hartsfield quipped: "This is the first time that I have ever had a whole horse in my office." When the zoo acquired its first male gorilla, the zoo director named him *Willie B.* in honor of the mayor. Hartsfield was very fond of *Willie B.* and took visitors out to the zoo to meet him. When the mayor ran *Willie B.* for congress against the incumbent Atlanta congressman, *Willie B.* didn't mind losing the election but was highly indignant when the congressman stated that "*Willie B.* was the usual caliber of his opposition."

But the sunny days of Atlanta's growth and prosperity were beginning to be threatened by the dark clouds of racial unrest. We have all been destined to live in a time when vast conflicts between nations have been replaced by continuing, cultural, religious, and racial warfare among people living in the same country or region, and usually fought-out within cities. In the Hartsfield time in Southern cities like Birmingham such strife was inevitable. City warfare raged in Belfast and Beirut in the years following.

Hartsfield realized before anyone else that the crucial battle over civil rights would be fought in Atlanta. The city, thanks largely to him, was the new capital of the old states of the Confederacy. The Second Battle of Atlanta would have as great an impact in this war as in 1864.

When in contact with mayors of other cities at home and abroad, Mayor Hartsfield was often challenged about the South's racial backwardness and he felt that people outside the South thought that Southerners were really an inferior, second-class group of Americans. He was stung by this prevailing attitude and found it difficult to explain to outsiders that the South was making substantial progress in race relations when the national and world press vibrated with the news of Southern lynchings, church dynamitings, and quoted Southern governors and senators urging *massive resistance.*

Being disinclined to defend such Southern practices by insisting that the press only highlighted the bad things dotting the Dixie landscape and none of the good things (the typical Segregationist lament and theme song of the day) he began to try and separate what was happening in Atlanta from the rest of the South. To get the story across that Atlanta was a different kind of Southern place. This was for the benefit of the city's image and for the benefit of the people who lived in Atlanta, for if he could not get the point across that an all-out fight against change would be bad for the city, then increasingly white Atlantans would become disenchanted with giving up old Segregationist ways. Hartsfield began to stand away from the mold which seemed to have shaped all other Southern politicians. In doing so, he brought Atlanta along with him.

The first step toward eventual Desegregation was the hiring of black police officers. Not merely the employment but the actual training and acceptance of these men as officers.

When Dad was named chief of police in January, 1947, he had the backing of Mayor Hartsfield and the City Council, and the press had been generous in its support, and Ralph McGill, editor of the Atlanta *Constitution,* wrote in his daily column that the city was in the mood to see changes and improvements within the police department. The Jewish community vigorously supported the change because Superintendent Fred Beerman, who was Jewish, was named the second highest officer in the department. This was a situation that occurred in no other Southern place.

The first thing Dad did was to get the state legislature to pass a law giving the chief of police in Atlanta full authority to hire, promote, and transfer all members of the department at his discretion and without having to seek the concurrence of any individual or governing body. Prior to this, the police committee of City Council had exercised that authority.

Next he had the entire police department re-structured and in the process abolished the position of assistant chief. Whenever a member of the City Council wanted to promote a supporter or relative within the department he would get him appointed an assistant chief. There were a number of them in the department all of whom were Klan members or sympathizers. This rather large contingent of highly placed personnel infiltrated every section, squad, and watch in the department and as such formed an impenetrable bulwark against modernizing the police department and the hiring of black officers.

It was a struggle to get these people out of power, and the Klan sued in court over the matter—and lost. This action essentially eliminated Klan influence in decision making in the police department.

For the next quarter of a century there would be only one chief on the police department reservation and whenever anyone spoke to, of, or about the "chief" there was absolutely no doubt in the mind of any Atlantan of whom the individual was speaking.

In all the years that Dad had known Mrs. Marsh, he had called her Peggy, but now like all other Atlantans he called her Margaret; and although she had called him Herbert in the past she now called him Chief, as did everyone else. It astonished me how readily they both assumed the new identity and discarded the old.

Before black officers could be hired the Mayor and City Council had to approve. When the Chief decided to move on the matter he did so quickly. The police committee had to hold a public hearing on the matter and did so beginning at 8:00 P.M. on a Wednesday. The hearing ran into the wee hours of the morning and all those who testified before the committee were vehemently against the employment of African-Americans as Atlanta Police Officers.

A number of the members of City Council insisted upon having a letter from the chief of police urging them to approve the employment of black police officers and stating that he could make it work. When they received the letter a vote on the resolution was taken and the measure managed to pass.

It was necessary for white Atlantans to change their way of thinking once Atlanta police officers of color were hired. Fortunately a thin majority of Atlantans were able to do so.

In this time a number of dignitaries visited Atlanta and Mayor Hartsfield would fete them to a parade and reception at the Georgian Terrace Hotel.

At one of these galas, I think it was the reception for Lady Astor, I was standing in the hotel ballroom when I felt someone tugging at me from behind. When I turned around I discovered a very exasperated Margaret Mitchell and John Marsh.

"Will you please—" And then she gasped for breath. "Will you please get your father's attention? We've been trying to talk to him—but he moves around so fast—I've never seen so many people! Where on earth did they all come from?" She and John were already holding onto one another so I took her hand and the three of us made a beeline for my Dad and if anyone was in our way I nudged them aside. This created a bit of a stir but when people realized who was coming through, got out of the way. The Marshes had been trying to be inconspicuous and avoid being recognized, and now my actions had caused everybody to realize who they were, but with some effort I managed to get them over to Dad and had them sandwiched between the people he had been talking with and himself. Both he and the other people looked at me sternly, but they sort of melted backwards when they realized who I had in tow.

When she could get her breath, Mrs. Marsh engaged my father in conversation, as John nodded his agreement.

"Like I was telling Mayor Bill on the phone yesterday, John and I want you to know that we fully support what you are doing in the police department. I know you have opposition . . . John and I hear it all the time, and I know you do too, but we are behind you one-hundred per cent!!"

The lady who had been talking to Dad could not contain herself any longer.

"Oh Mrs. Mitchell! Oh Mrs. Mitchell! Oh Mrs. Mitchell I just can't believe that it is really you!!!" She gushed.

"And Mr. Mitchell too!!!!" She squealed as she grabbed John Marsh's hand and began pumping it as though she were drilling for oil.

The crowd was pressing in upon us and Dad hastily signaled for backup. Several uniformed officers quickly came to the rescue and escorted the Marshes safely away.

I never saw Margaret Mitchell again. She died soon afterwards at the age of forty-nine from injuries she suffered when hit by a car while crossing Peachtree Street. But there has never been any doubt in my mind about where she stood on the race issue.

When the first eight black Atlanta police officers completed their training and were outfitted in their uniforms, issued badges and guns, Dad and Mayor Hartsfield led them in a parade march along Decatur Street. I was in the crowd along the sidewalk watching the procession go by and it was a chilly winter day and everybody was moving about and trying to keep warm and many in the crowd had celebrated the occasion with strong drink.

As the new policemen marched by in front of us a man in the crowd ran up to the shortest of the policemen and began hollering:

"Look at the mouse!!! Look at the mouse!!! Look at the mouse!!!" But barely got going good when this beefy man in the crowd darted out and grabbed the protestor by the neck and dragged him back to the sidewalk and dumped him down on the cement as though he were a sack of potatoes. Everybody cheered.

Due to careful planning, and despite an ongoing dissent by a large minority of white Atlantans, the new policemen performed in their new jobs so well that we were all astounded at how quickly this change in the Southern way of living had occurred. But soon the Segregationist's would come up with their program of *massive resistance.*

At the same time that African-Americans were being hired as police officers, Branch Rickey brought Jackie Robinson into the major leagues to play for the Brooklyn Dodgers. It has always struck me as ironic that it was a baseball manager and a Southern police chief who were willing to go farther than anyone else before them to end discrimination in America.

The Fountain and its pre-grown Magnolia trees and City Auditorium

The State Capitol–top left, the Atlanta City Hall with flag flying.
The Amen Corner, hidden by trees, is to the east of City Hall.

The Chief and Margie

The Chief eargerly promoting
his Native American Heritage

Strange Interlude

Atlanta's First Black Officers
(seated left to right) H.H. Hooks, Claude Dickson, E.H. Lyons
(standing left to right) Robert McKibbens, Willard W. Strickland,
W.T. Elkins, Johnnie P. Jones, John Sanders

School Traffic Policewomen reported for
duty, March 6, 1950; TOP ROW: Mamie
Wiggins - Sarah Greene - Myrtis Rawls
BOTTOM ROW: Emma Hughley -
Mayme Bondu - Nellie Sellers

The author at the podium in the United States House of
Representatives the day General Douglas MacArthur spoke
April 19, 1951

The Chief and Mayor with Miss
Nell (Mrs. Robert W. Woodruff)
Ichauway Plantation
January, 1952

Lillian Smith, author, and
outspoken opponent of
Segregation in the South
in the 1950s

Mayor

Helen Bullard with Q.V. Williamson - the first African-American
Bullard got elected to the Atlanta City Council

Godfather
Robert W. Woodruff

A
RECOGNITION DINNER

honoring

DR. MARTIN LUTHER KING, JR.
CITIZEN OF ATLANTA

Winner of the

1964 NOBEL PEACE PRIZE

Sponsored by
CITIZENS OF ATLANTA

JANUARY 27TH

DINKLER PLAZA HOTEL   •   ATLANTA, GEORGIA

7 O'CLOCK

PROGRAM

NOBEL PEACE PRIZE DINNER

Greetings by Rabbi Jacob Rothschild

The National Anthem

The Invocation by Rev. Samuel Williams

Introduction of Dais Guests

Dinner

Music by Morehouse College Choir

Tributes
Mayor Ivan Allen, Jr.

Bishop Ernest L. Hickman

·Rev. Edward A. Driscoll

Senator Leroy Johnson

Archbishop Paul J. Hallinan

Introduction of Honoree by Dr. Benjamin E. Mays

Address—Dr. Martin Luther King, Jr.

Presentation of Gift

Benediction by Rev. Ralph Abernathy

Pericles's Parthenon
(as reproduced in Nashville, TN)

Hartsfield's Hartsfield
(the year he left office)

Hartsfield International Airport

E Buford Dam Hartsfield's legacy to future generations.

The Author

Jennifer and Jay
niece and nephew

Margie

SIXTEEN

VOM WINDE VERWEHT

The rise of Hitler in Germany is a phenomenon that had an enormous impact on ending Segregation in the South because it influenced the thinking of many influential Atlantans.

One such person, who I got to know during the time of the employment of African-American police officers, and the only woman who could be considered a part of the red-hot-center of the Desegretation saga in Atlanta, was Helen Bullard.

Bullard came to Atlanta out of the *Deliverance* country of North Georgia via the University of Georgia and the University of Chicago. That a young girl from the Georgia mountains would study on a Rosenwald Fellowship at the Yankee school that Southerners who at that time had heard of it deemed it to be a breeding ground for Communist radicals, tells us a great deal about this indomitable woman whose profession in Atlanta for four decades would have to be termed advertising and public relations.

Although Bullard did her time selling soap, soon upon reaching Atlanta it became obvious that she was destined for a higher calling. Since she grew up in North Georgia she was from a section of the state far removed from the tradition of plantation culture or the cotton-dominated way of thinking. At the University of Chicago her natural inclinations and liberal outlook were urbanized.

Bullard equated the rise of Hitler in Germany with what could have happened in this country if concerned and educated people had not become involved in politics as the issue of Desegregation came to the forefront of the social and political scene. Early on in her time in Atlanta she got very involved in reform-minded Atlanta politics. In the late thirties and forties Atlanta Desegregation activists were a small group of Southern-born, Protestant white women who regarded Georgia author Lillian Smith as their spiritual leader. Helen Bullard was the field general.

With a talent for promoting that would have made Ivy Lee look bad, Bullard began selling Desegregation at a time in the South when such a program was well nigh unthinkable. But Bullard insisted that people had to get involved. Segregation had to end. The problem could not be left to the Klan. Look at what happened in Germany.

Knowing full well that most older white Southerners were beyond hope on the subject, she began by working with the younger folk. There are countless prominent Atlantans and others now living throughout the country, who first began to question the ideas of black and white with which they grew up, when as college students they had been herded into Amen Corner church basements at one of Bullard's endless seminars on the racial problem.

She would bring in Northern speakers sometimes, but usually she would have a small group of blacks from a church or a group from one of the black colleges in Atlanta stand up and tell the meeting what it was like to be treated as a second-class citizen in the city of Atlanta.

For people who had gone through grade school, high school, and college and never questioned or been challenged by teachers or professors about their racial attitudes, Bullard's church basement seminars were eye-openers. If she did not change people's minds right off, that was okay. She succeeded in creating a dialogue on the subject, and this was something new for Atlanta.

With the coming of black participation in the electorial process, Bullard expanded her activities. The meetings in white churches now included meetings in black churches. Groups of whites got up and told how they never knew what it was like for blacks. As the dialogue grew and expanded, political awareness accelerated.

Soon most of Bullard's time was being spent in managing political campaigns, and although in the beginning the candidates that the new white/black coalition supported and that Bullard managed were hardly Integrationists, the individual was usually a better *hope* than the candidate he was opposing.

Campaign money was hard to come by but Bullard soon became a pro in getting local businessmen to give a small contribution. She stressed that it was their responsibility to be involved in politics, and to run for office. Many of those who contributed money would probably never have done so had not Bullard been onto them first to run for elective office. This effort began to get some few more enlightened people elected to city and country offices.

In 1952, Bullard's coalition elected Dr. Rufus Clement, the President of Atlanta University, to the city school board on a city-wide ballot. Dr. Clement had the distinction of being the first black man elected to political office in the South since Reconstruction.

By the end of World War II, Bullard was managing Hartsfield's campaigns and bringing the support of her constituency to the reform programs which the mayor exposed. Indeed, she was a strong voice in shaping those programs.

"The've burned Lillian out." Helen's voice on the phone was agitated and concerned. "But no one was home. They burned her house in the night while she was away. But all her papers—everything is a total loss."

We were on our way to North Georgia in no time flat. I was thinking with somewhat large guilt that at long last I would get to meet author Lillian Smith.

Lillian Smith was born in a small town in Florida but moved to the North Georgia mountains with her family as a youngster. Her father operated a Summer camp for teenagers.

Lillian went off to college, wrote articles condemning Segregation in the South, and lived in China. When her father died she returned to North Georgia and operated her father's Summer camp. When she took over along with horseback riding, swimming, and campfire building she included courses in art and literature and sensitivity instruction on the racial issue. Segregationist politicians called her camp a breeding ground for communist radicals.

Lillian Smith was the pre-eminent voice in the South for social change. She was the Ida Tarbell in the fight against Segregation. For the younger generation of rebels she was our champion.

We walked among the ruins and shook our heads and made quiet comments on the total destruction of Lillian's home. That unmistakable smell of intense heat fueled by gasoline hung heavily over the mound of ashes which had been Lillian's home. The all too familiar odor I first smelled when the home of a black family in a previously all-white Atlanta neighborhood was torched. It would invade my nostrils again and again as firebombings in the South accelerated.

"This was my house, my life, my everything," Lillian intoned quietly. We had all gathered at the camp where Lillian had taken up temporary residence. Other people had driven in to view the damage and brought linens and dishes and offered condolences to Lillian. It was like a death in the family of which Southern writers are always writing so movingly.

"But—I'm all right—I will go on and, thank goodness, my article for Life was already in the mail." There were sighs of approval from the group.

"Containment. Containment. What has happened here is not all that important—merely in a personal way to me—but what we must do is work harder to contain the fire to this mountaintop; we must stamp it out here or else it will spread all over Georgia, all over the South, all over America and the country will burn down through the decades well nigh on into the next century . . ." Very, very prophetic words as things turned out. All we have to do is flick on the TV news channel to realize that Lillian knew whereof she spoke.

Had the evening concluded on this laudable plain then Helen and my visit to North Georgia would have been on a par with Moses ascending the mountaintop. But alas, the Bible was so tome-filled there were no pages left to record who said what to whom afterwards. Not so on this occasion.

Later in the evening, Helen and I were having a private conversation with Lillian, recounting the details of the battle then going on in Atlanta. Atlanta politics was Helen's lifeblood. Lillian listened politely but at times her interest flagged and her eyes darted about the room.

In a lull in the conversation, and in an attempt to pep things up and make my speech and say to Lillian Smith what I had rehearsed for all of my young lifetime to say to this eminent Georgia writer who I idolized completely, I recounted to her how in the Summertime in the Indian Fields at the Mason homeplace, Eva and I ran a lending library for family and friends and how that after reading *Strange Fruit* we decided it was just too radical for our clientele and we had concealed Lillian's book inside the dust jacket of *Kings Row*.

I might as well have thrown a firebomb on the conversation, for Lillian appeared highly offended by the story and quickly faded away. I looked at Helen in despair.

"You don't know as much as you think you know," Helen

commented dryly. "No matter what else, writers are always writers first."

Lillian Smith had been one of the first Southern women to be awarded a Rosenwald scholarship to study at the University of Chicago. Afterwards she was a member of the recruitment committee which awarded a scholarship to Helen Bullard.

The two Southern women were much alike in some ways; quite different in others. Intellectual, gifted, girlish in appearance, flirtatious when they needed to be to get their own way, yet also the very first dedicated feminists in the South. And whereas all her life Lillian maintained her constant girlhood weight and presented a persona of the thin, iconoclastic, leader of the revolution telling the world by her appearance that it was evil to be fat when there was so much oppression in the world and those in the leadership to make the world a better place should project an image of lean thought and body, Helen, to the contrary, seemed to gain weight with each passing year.

For Southern women of their generation smoking cigarettes was mandatory because it was the most visible sign of female independence.

Helen smoked constantly and even way back then people cautioned her that it was a health hazard. If she commented at all it was usually to say:

"Hitler never smoked and would not allow anyone in his presence to smoke. He said it was the worst thing a person could do."

Before we departed and after Lillian and Helen discussed the world situation at length and smoked all their own cigarettes and all those of other people in the room, Lillian had to bring up Helen's weight problem. Nobody in Atlanta would do such a thing but then nobody in Atlanta had Lillian's status as the apostle of change.

On the return trip to Atlanta Helen had a lot to say about the short-sightedness of visionaries.

While World War II was still raging overseas, the Reverend Clarence Jordan and his wife Florence, had founded the 1,400 acre Christian community they christened Koinonia (Coin-uh-NEE-uh) Farm. This remarkable white couple practiced Christlike poverty, preached nonviolence and racial tolerance, and worked to provide social services for those individuals in need regardless of race.

Helen absolutely adored the Jordans and had raised money

for them. She had been involved with Koinonia from the beginning and helped the Reverend Jordan get free legal assistance from a sympathetic Atlanta lawyer.

By the mid-fifties the most inflammatory word in Georgia was not Communism but Koinonia. The farm was located in the heart of the old Confederacy just outside Americus, Georgia. President Jimmy Carter's hometown of Plains was nearby.

Once again Helen and I journeyed out of Atlanta on an inspection trip to view the destruction to property caused by the accelerating racial crisis. Far and away, the damage at Koinonia was vaster than that suffered by Lillian Smith.

Reverend Jordan conducted us on a tour of the farm and it was like viewing a war zone. The KKK had come in the night and burned buildings and destroyed farm equipment. Farm animals had been trapped and burned alive. This time the smell of gasoline ignited debris was intermixed with the odor of burned and rotting flesh.

The enormity of the devastation moved Helen into action. Reverend Jordan's stance in favor of Desegregated schools had led to this latest and worst of several outrages committed against Koinonia. School children from the farm were being regularly beaten up at school and on the school bus. For Helen, it was Nazi Germany all over again.

Using her network of forward-thinking individuals in Atlanta and fanning out all over the state, she managed to play a behind the scenes role with the good folks of Georgia to take a stand against violence.

On several trips we made to rural Georgia, Helen met with town leaders, and, seated at a large dining table or an oil-cloth covered kitchen table, she preached to them the message she had been selling to Atlanta for nearly two decades: Violence can provide the opportunity for good people to take a stand against mob rule. With few women in the groups, most of the round-table participants were all white men who had been born, reared, and expected to die under the system of Segregation. It was Helen's job to convince this reluctant assemblage that they must change their way of thinking, and then, more importantly, use their influence to persuade others to do likewise.

To see Helen at the negotiating table doing what at this point in time she had been doing so long that she now did better than anyone else in the South, was a revelation.

With her page-boy haircut, vise-like eye contact, a voice that one minute vibrated like a harp and the next rose to organesque indignation in a manner that any opera singer would envy, and her exquisite hands invading the air space with the skill of a Maestro, her audience was both titillated and mesmerized. She was a performer who worked magic upon her listeners and she persuaded many of the leaders in the small towns throughout Georgia to begin speaking out against violence.

On our nighttime return to Atlanta, we were always tailgated by local police hoping to nab us for some infraction of the traffic laws—Helen and I hanging out the windows in search of prevailing speed limit signs. In hindsight, to our pursuers, we must have seemed like two lost aliens from another planet.

The legacy of Koinonia survives because President Jimmy Carter and others in Georgia were influenced by its high ideals and launched the worldwide Habitat For Humanity organization which Jimmy and Rosalyn Carter have done so much to encourage since leaving the White House, and thanks to their untiring efforts Habitat For Humanity is an organization that has grown to encompass eight-hundred cities in thirty-seven countries.

We had all gathered in the mayor's office at City Hall. It was a send-off conclave: The Mayor was going on a tour of Europe and I was leaving to go to Washington to become a page in the United States House of Representatives.

The Mayor had a stack of autographed copies of *GWTW* which he was going to take with him, and I had inveigled upon him to let me have several. They were, of course, fakes. Margaret Mitchell had died suddenly and had been adverse to signing copies of her book anyway, and the Mayor had none to bestow upon dignitaries. He had begun the practice of having his secretary autograph copies of *GWTW* and she did a marvelous job of faking the author's signature.

Mother had been close to Margaret Mitchell because, among other things, she was Ellery and Almanza's granddaughter. At the functions the two of them would have long conversations and when I would inquire of Mother afterwards what they were talking about, she would look at me and say nonchalantly:

"Oh, just girl talk. Nothing you would be interested in. Certainly not anything for you to write down in that journal of yours."

My journal, urged upon me by my elders as a means of broadening my education, was now viewed by many of those close to me as some kind of threat and I believe they would think twice about saying things they knew I would record. Each passing day our world became more tense.

Mother had excoriated the Mayor at some length about the immorality of the faked autographs. She insisted it was wrong and an insult to Margaret Mitchell's memory. To my surprise the Mayor did not answer her back, for it was not his nature to let an attack on his morality go unchallenged, and rather meekly, and for him I thought uncharacteristically so, he said that he never ever did this for Atlantans, but only for foreign visitors. He went on to say that the people in Western Europe had endured so much and lost so much that he was sure Margaret Mitchell would be the first to approve of his actions.

"Nothing, and I mean nothing, can bring happiness into the eyes of someone who lived and suffered through World War II, than receiving an autographed copy of *GWTW*. And who are we to deny people such a wonderful gift simply because of a tragic automobile accident?"

"But you can simply give them a copy of the book—It doesn't have to—what you are doing diminishes the book."

"Its not the same," the Mayor responded, and he changed the subject. He did, however, discontinue the practice.

It was strange to see mother and the Mayor going at it and being in disagreement on something. They were nearly always in accord.

What had been planned as a bon voyage evening had turned out a bit sticky. Earlier in the evening, we had attended the annual banquet of the department heads of the city of Atlanta. This group met over lunch once a month and once a year had a banquet at a downtown hotel and all the wives attended as did the council members and their wives.

Upon this occasion, and at the conclusion of his talk, Mayor Hartsfield spoke about the racial issue and how the South would have to change peaceably and that Atlanta must lead the way. He ended by saying:

"And in this I want you all to look toward the Chief and Mrs. Marge—for in this regard they are on the right wavelength on the racial issue and they can be a tremendous help to all of you in your departments and to us in Atlanta if we all work together and follow their example."

If Helen and I had not been seated at a table in the back to lead off what turned out to be purely perfunctory applause, the

Mayor's remarks would have been received in total silence.

As the meeting broke up everyone wished the Mayor a pleasant and productive journey—pointedly ignoring his comments on the racial issue. Afterwards there were some council members and their wives who never again spoke to my mother or father or attended any function where they were present, and, if by chance found themselves in their presence, immediately departed.

Thus the reason for the testiness in the office of the Mayor later that night. As we groped for answers everyone talked at once except Helen, who sat quietly, puffing away. Finally she entered the conversation.

"It is the closing of the Southern mind on the question of race, the pretending that it does not exist. Tonight William Berry (Helen always called Hizzoner William Berry) you made them confront the issue, and for some of them for the first time in their lives—we are lucky, I believe, that at least they did not throw any of that overcooked, rubbery, chicken at you all," and Helen and I roared with laughter but no one else did.

Helen had written the Mayor's speech for that evening, and as usual, he put it aside and spoke without a script. He was superb at seeming to speak (Ronald Reagan without a teleprompter) extemporaneously, while in fact, as I learned when I looked over the written copy of Helen's speech, he had given the last part verbatim as she had written it, and she was not upset by the audience's lack of enthusiasm.

"I really don't see why you all are so surprised by the negative reaction, for it was, in fact, a good beginning. We will simply turn up the heat next time and then they will be begging to hear again what they did not want to hear tonight."

The Mayor was driving (neither the Mayor or the Chief ever had a driver) Helen home and a stranger would have assumed the two were husband and wife from the way that Helen gazed upon, and talked to, Hizzoner. It was obvious to everyone that he was the love of her life, but in fact Helen was unmarried and the Mayor had been married to the same woman for many years.

Mrs. Hartsfield never liked politics and as the years went by took less interest in being the mayor's wife and behaved as though she was married to an ordinary citizen.

When racial tension increased, and Mrs. Hartsfield began to get anonymous phone calls at home from people who asked her what was it like to be married to an Integrationist, she retreated from public life altogether.

That Autumn, I had first come to realize that Dad was using me to defend Desegregation.

People went to church on Sunday, and in the Fall on Saturday afternoon to the football game to watch Georgia Tech wallop their usually hapless opponent. Both were a religion in Atlanta.

Prior to the game one Saturday afternoon the epitome of Southern male macho supreme, a man who was idolized like a god by everyone in Atlanta, accosted me and let me know in no uncertain terms what he thought of me and what he obviously had heard and concluded I was all about.

"You think you are one of those people who know everything—but you are not. People like you want to change things because you can't make it in the world the way it is, and, for your information, the South is the greatest place on earth!!"

For my part, I made no reply and tried to sort of fade into the lengthening afternoon shadows.

Somewhat astonished by the source of the outburst it was not something I had not heard before. My Dad was always saying to anyone and everyone that the younger generation wanted a change in the social situation in the South. When pressed, he always quoted me as the source of this new sentiment.

This tended to disarm the opposition. Few individuals wanted to tell the chief of police his son was an idiot. But as I found out they had absolutely no compunction in telling me.

To the point where on the other side of the coin as it were and on another occasion when I discovered that no less than Robert Woodruff, who at this juncture in time was well on his way to becoming the Godfather of Atlanta, had approached me unawares, looked me straight in the eye, and said:

"There must be no let up, and you must keep up the pressure and you cannot go slack because if you go slack they will roll all over you . . ." I did sort of have that Alice in Wonderland feeling.

No doubt to the casual observer the South in this era appeared to be a place where people went about speaking in tongues. This was not the case at all. It was simply Southern curtain-closing. There was only one issue in the South then, and everybody knew that, and words were used as a coverup because it was much too painful to speak about the matter openly.

SEVENTEEN

CAPITOL HILL HIGH

In the nation's capital, the 82nd Congress churned onward. My days as a page in the United States House of Representatives in the fading months of the Truman Administration were numbered, but the many visitors from back home continued unabated.

The House had failed to pass in full the appropriation bill for funding to build the Buford Dam on the Chattahoochee River north of Atlanta. Building the dam and creating a giant reservoir was absolutely essential to provide an adequate water supply for the region. Without construction of the Buford Dam Atlanta had no chance of ever becoming a major American City.

Mayor Hartsfield would not accept the fact that all the time he had spent in Washington that year would come to naught. During this time I was beginning to think that my entire life was to be laced with this ongoing struggle over Atlanta's future water needs.

Once again, Mayor Hartsfield was in the capitol and had commandeered my services in helping him discuss the issue with Georgia's most well-known senator.

Although the appropriation bill which passed the House had slashed funding for the Buford Dam, when the bill reached the Senate floor, the entire funding for the project had been restored.

Now the bill was slated to go to conference. If Georgia's Senator Richard Russell, the chairman of the Senate Appropriations Committeee, could succeed in conference with the House leaders in keeping full funding for the Buford Dam in the appropriation bill, then approval by both Houses of Congress would be perfunctory. Thus the question of whether or not the dam would

become a reality depended upon the action taken by the conference committee. The man who controlled that committee was
Senator Russell.

I had been around the Congress long enough to know that if
Senator Russell wanted the Buford Dam in the bill it would be
in the bill.

Mayor Hartsfield was a persuasive salesman. Due primarily to
his efforts, Senator Russell had agreed to sponsor the bill and
gotten it passed in the Senate.

On paper, it would appear that his action was on behalf of a
political ally, for Hartsfield was the Democratic mayor of Georgia's largest city, and Russell was the state's most noted Democratic member of the United States Congress. In reality, there
was an abyss between the Mayor and the Senator as wide as the
Grand Canyon. This gulf was created by the question of race.

African-Americans were beginning to vote in large numbers,
particularly in Atlanta precincts where they had no trouble getting registered. This was cause for alarm for Senator Russell and
his supporters many of whom viewed Atlanta as an alien space
station plunked down right in the middle of the green pastures
and Segregated cotton fields of Georgia.

As I walked across the Senate floor, I observed Senator Russell seated at his desk on the center aisle. He had just about the
best seat in the Senate and at that point in time it seemed to
belong to him by divine right.

It had been an exceptional congressional session and Senator
Russell had played the starring role. The special Senate committee designated to investigate the firing of General Douglas Mac-
Arthur by President Truman had been chaired by Senator Russell. For his conduct in this difficult task, Senator Russell had
been applauded by members from both sides of the aisle and
since the hearings were among the first televised, had become a
national figure, and, with the possible exception of Republican
Senators Taft and Joe McCarthy, the most well-recognized
member of the United States Senate.

I approached Senator Russell in the best congressional-page-
training manner I could muster. I had learned that the one facet
of the page persona most cherished by members of congress was
eagerness. Always be eager: Eager to please, eager to serve, eager
to learn.

When I was assigned to write a paper for school which had to
include an interview with a member of congress, I managed to

persuade Senator Russell to be interviewed on the General Mac-
Arthur committee hearings, a rather successful effort as it
turned out in which I compared Russell favorably to Robert E.
Lee for which I received my highest grade ever for a school
assignment.

Nothing flattered a page school teacher so much as having a
paper to grade for which one of the nation's more notable distinguished senators had provided an interview.

That's not to imply that page school teachers were more susceptible to flattery than anyone else in this Holy City of political
indulgencies. It applied to everyone and those with the most
power were most exposed to its influence, and sometimes
conversion.

As always, Senator Russell was the essence of old-time Southern politeness when I informed him that the mayor of Atlanta
awaited him outside the Senate chamber. Unlike previous times,
when he had me place Hartsfield in an anteroom and kept the
mayor waiting for hours until he saw him, this time he immediately arose from his desk to go to meet with the mayor.

I sensed right away that the senator's buoyant attitude bode
well for Hartsfield and the city of Atlanta and I was giddy with
excitement as I accompanied Senator Russell up the center aisle
of the Senate.

But to leave no stone unturned as it were, I told Senator Russell of what a success the MacArthur interview had been and
had left it in his office for his perusal—when he had the time, of
course.

As I swung open the massive door of the chamber for the Senator, he was absolutely beaming as he and Hartsfield enthusias-
tically shook hands and then quickly vanished into a nearby
room to seal the fate of Atlanta's future.

I felt really let down as I worked my way through a throng of
camera-clacking tourists on my way back to the House side of
the capitol. The trouble with being a junior political manipula-
tor was that in spite of all your toil, you never got to witness the
end of the story. You were forever excluded from the grand,
third act, finale.

The following afternoon I got a phone call from Dad. He had
just come from the mayor's office where the movers and shakers
of Atlanta were holding a victory celebration. Senator Russell
had assured Hartsfield that full funding for the Buford Dam
would pass the Congress this session. Preliminary planning for

the dam could begin right away. The project, so vital for Atlanta's growth, was assured.

But the deciding factor in Senator Russell's decision to make the Buford Dam dream become a reality, had little to do with Atlanta. The actual sight of the dam and the huge reservoir which would supply water for Atlanta well into the 21st century, happen to lie in the very heart of the district of Senator Russell's closest political allies; when completed, the lake would practically adjoin the Senator's hometown.

Many Russell supporters owned farm land in the area: Land which had been overfarmed for generations, was in many instances abandoned to scrub pine, and in the years following World War II deemed to be of scant monetary value. When the landowners learned that the government was willing to pay top dollar to secure the property, they were anxious to sell and urged Senator Russell to bring the project to Georgia.

Thus, one of the vital elements for Atlanta's growth came about not because a powerful political leader wanted to lay the foundation for the building of a great city, but to please his unconcerned political supporters residing in the agrarian Southland.

The following week Dad was in D.C. to see Mr. Hoover at the FBI. In his efforts to modernize and upgrade the Atlanta Police Department, my Dad often had to turn to Hoover and the FBI for assistance. There was then no other organization in the country involved in modern law enforcement.

For his part, Hoover was glad to have an ally in the South where his FBI agents could operate without being shot at. In this era FBI agents were thought by Segregationist-minded Southern sheriffs and police officers to be left wing radicals bent on outlawing the Southern way of life. To the extent that the FBI was opposed to lynchings, the Ku Klux Klan, and other like-minded terrorist organizations in Dixie, they were quite right.

Dad suggested that I accompany him on his visit to the Bureau (when anyone in law enforcement mentioned the word 'Bureau' everyone knew he meant FBI) and meet the Director (everyone in Washington knew this meant Hoover) who even then was more than a legend because although there were many generals, admirals, representatives, and senators in D.C., there was but one Director.

As we entered the FBI building the musical score from the old radio show *Gangbusters* pounded silently in my brain. One becomes blasé to official Washington in time, but a visit to the man who nabbed Dillinger had an effect even upon my jaded sensibilities.

The Director was very pleasant and affable. He said he was delighted to make my acquaintance. His appearance lacked the granite-like facade that I had imagined, and he was far from being the imposing figure I had supposed. Not only that, but his office looked quite ordinary and was nothing like many of the grandiose offices in the Capitol. I was rather disappointed—and bored.

Hoover and Dad were discussing padded cells. Even that failed to spark my interest. Dad had struggled mightily to put an end to police brutality against those Atlantans being held in police custody.

It was then common practice for the police in America to beat the tar out of anyone and everyone just on general principle. It happened daily. No one who protested managed to change things. It was police procedure. But Dad had put a stop to it in Atlanta. He fired any officer on the spot who exhibited such behavior.

Now, the problem was, that people who were mentally impaired while incarcerated in the Atlanta city jail often did themselves bodily harm and even committed suicide.

Before the advent of behavior-correcting medication and adequate facilities to treat and house these people, they would end up in the city jail. Seemingly this was not a major police concern in any other American city, but Dad, ever the innovator in his field, was earnestly trying to find a solution to this problem. Therefore his interest in padded cells.

The Director assured him that there was no such thing as a padded cell anywhere in America. Except, of course, in the movies. End of the discussion.

My good friend Charles Bell, a page from Athens, Georgia, had a compelling interest in the world situation. He had wanted to be a page so that when he was older and had a career he could help make the world a better place. Such a high-minded attitude was rare in Washington in those days.

During the long late-night session the week before and debate on the Foreign Aid appropriation bill, both he and I discussed the issue at some length with Congressman John F. Kennedy of Massachusetts whose primary concern then was the world situation.

When I encountered Congressman Kennedy outside the House chamber, I introduced him to Dad.

Right off, Mr. Kennedy wanted to know what, in my Dad's opinion was the major police problem in the country.

"Having to enforce outdated Segregation laws. If we in the South do not move rapidly to abolish Segregation, there will be an assault upon the police power that will severely damage the country."

It was August, 1951, and Congressman Kennedy from his reaction had obviously never heard anyone, let alone a Southern police chief, speak so candidly on the racial issue.

"I, think, Chief, I would really like to hear more about this," and he and Dad vanished into an adjoining anteroom.

Where, to the surprise of both me and Charles Bell, they remained for the next two hours.

"What in the world were you and Mr. Kennedy discussing all that time?" I asked Dad later.

"Segregation. Segregation and what to do about it."

"For two hours?"

"Oh, we did touch on other matters."

"Like what?"

"Well, he was really interested in the Boston police strike. He told me his grandaddy had been mayor of Boston."

EIGHTEEN

KEEPING UP WITH PERICLES AND ASPASIA

Pericles: 495-429 B.C. Athenian statesman, orator, and foremost citizen. Under his leadership Athens became a glorious city.

Aspasia: Intimate companion of Pericles. He became devoted to her in middle age and depended upon her for advice and counsel. She was the most influential woman of the Periclean age.

I was rushing downtown headed for the city auditorium—on mid-semester break from school at Duke University.

Much pressure had been placed upon me to go to college in Atlanta where I would be more accessible but I wanted a broader based education and chose Duke University which turned out to be a wise choice because there I received instruction from Professor Harold Parker, a man of powerful intellect and history instructor who had a deep and profound impact upon the lives of countless numbers of Duke students.

From Dr. Parker's courses on the American, French, and Spanish American Revolutions and the Development of Modern Historical Thought I received the educational base I needed to help end Segregation in Atlanta.

Trackless trolleys, giant transit vehicles electrically powered by dual overhead voltage lines, had replaced Atlanta streetcars. On the up side the trolleys were quiet, clean, energy-saving, and would accommodate a large number of riders in each vehicle. On the down side the hugh pachyderms snarled traffic, were slow and cumbersome, and tended to lose contact with the overhead wires while tooling along Atlanta's hilly, twisting, boulevards.

I was aboard a trolley and it seemed destined not to ever move out of traffic gridlock; so, I exited the trolley and walked the remaining four blocks to the auditorium. It struck me as a peculiar means of travel to reach the starting point of a revolution but this was 20th century Atlanta and not 19th century Bolivia. And for that I was eternally grateful.

To the hundreds of riot-ready state troopers ringing the entrance of the city auditorium the sight of a lone white boy clad in a blue blazer, gray-flanneled slacks, button-down collar shirt and striped tie and cordovan loafers—the preppie uniform of the day—must have appeared as an outlandish and out-of-place mirage as I rushed toward the auditorium where the national convention of the National Association for the Advancement of Colored People (NAACP) was already in progress.

As I raced up the steps there was a derisive roar from a crowd of angry whites across the street waving obscene banners who had invaded Hartsfield's beloved park. Some of them ended up falling into the fountain as the crowd pushed against the police barrier in hopes of being able to force their way inside and disrupt the meeting, but a sturdy force of Atlanta police held them at bay.

I grasped the increasing discontent of the *massive resistance* movement when I saw, for the first time the confederate flag being waved by several of the protestors, and realized that the other side was indeed determined to stage a second Battle of Atlanta.

As I entered the outer door and moved toward the doors leading directly into the auditorium my way was blocked by a rotund Atlanta policeman who had known me all my life—

"Now you don't really want to be going in there—" he was saying— But without thinking and never breaking stride, I swiftly moved around him and pushed against an adjoining door which thankfully flew open and I ran right onto the floor of the convention and took a seat on the next to last row.

After getting my bearings, I saw Eliza Paschall seated down the row with some of her colleagues and we exchanged greetings. Eliza was the Executive Director of the Greater Atlanta Council On Human Relations. Her organization was an essential element of the liberal bi-racial political coalition which Helen created.

Eliza Paschall was the widow of Walter Paschall whose father had been editor of the Atlanta *Journal*. Both Eliza and Walter Paschall were pioneers working to change things in Atlanta and the South and when Walter died at an early age from a sudden heart attack, his widow carried on the work the two of them had begun.

The NAACP had chosen Atlanta because it wished to meet in the South and felt that Atlanta was the only city where it would be safe. There were plenty of people in government who would have liked to have seen it turn into a convention of violence. Mayor Hartsfield was determined that it would not, for the press was here from all over the country to cover the convention. Many veiled threats and some not so veiled were received by practically all city officials who had anything to do with the convention.

The Governor was denouncing the NAACP and Atlanta for allowing the convention to assembly here. The atmosphere was tense and ominous. State troopers had been called into Atlanta and they drove around the capital, city hall, and had massed outside the auditorium.

Mayor Hartsfield was hell-bent to clear the atmosphere. His entrance into the hall to give the welcoming address to the convention was greeted with wild and enthusiastic applause.

Right off, he *dared* any agitators or anyone else to create any violence while the convention was in session. It was the most courageous speech he ever gave and only a person with his guts could have made it. I felt so proud to be an Atlantan.

Hartsfield's strong offensive caused those who were inclined to make trouble to back off and then to leave town because the Mayor made it abundantly clear that the city would severely deal with any trouble makers.

The Mayor's tough address upon this occasion also caused those advocating *massive resistance* to back down. Not only were the agitators departing the city, but the state troopers who had been massing in such large numbers began leaving. It was an historic speech by Hartsfield because it turned a city which was on the brink of violence completely around.

By the last days of the convention no one was even noticing that the NAACP was in town. It was a fierce act of courage, but one that Mayor Hartsfield thought perfectly ordinary because Atlanta, his city, was being threatened. In such an atmosphere a bear defending its cubs could not have been more menacing. But it was, all things considered, a rather typical event during this hectic era, for we were all called upon to do things we had never done before.

"I just hate this place," Helen was muttering under her

breath. We were seated at a luncheon at the Piedmont Driving Club. It was the most famous such club in Atlanta and then the undisputed headquarters of Atlanta Society.

"I just hate this place. Everytime I have to come here I dislike it all the more."

I was eying Helen wonderingly, as everybody in the room, except Helen, was eating away, thoroughly enjoying the food.

"Why don't you like it here?" I inquired. "It is certainly your kind of food," I insisted as I chomped down on the turnip greens and corn muffins and washed it all down with clinking iced tea. The entire room was clinking and chewing and chatting away, save Helen, who looked glum and merely picked at her food.

"Here, try some of this sweet potato soufflé it will melt in your mouth— Oh, and look, hot rolls!!" I shrieked in delight as I took several from the gleaming silver tray being passed by the immaculately attired waiter.

These were the wealthiest people in Atlanta but they ate just like the kitchen help. From time to time attempts had been made to, how shall we say it— modernize—the food offerings at the Piedmont Driving Club but it always failed; and the membership demanded the return of regular food and whether you call it soul food, Southern cooking, or regional cuisine it's basically all the same. There were separate races in the South, a Segregated social system, rich people and the not so rich, the bosses and the workers, but everyone ordered off the same menu in this era—and preferred it that way.

I was mystified as to why Helen was so morose but thought she was probably still unhappy by the outcome of our luncheon the week before at a downtown men's club.

We had labored long and hard on the right speech for Hizzoner to deliver to this organization composed mainly of the heads of local businesses and middle-level managers of large companies, a group of men many already approaching retirement age and nearly all hardliners on the subject of Desegregation.

You might well ask— then why was the Mayor speaking before this group? For one thing, the Mayor insisted on doing so. He liked to take the battle right into the enemy's camp and although he knew many of these men personally few had ever voted for him in the past and he was eager to change all that by speaking to them in their own language— explaining to them that the determination to hang onto Segregation would be bad for business, whereas, on the other hand, if Atlanta led the way to end years of oppression it would be very good for business.

I had arrived at the meeting and joined Helen at a table in the back of the dining room. I could scarcely believe my eyes because Helen who always wore colorful clothing and never wore a hat even in this era when few Atlanta women appeared in public hatless, was dressed in a plain navy blue suit and matching blue straw hat. The hat was round without any kind of ornamentation and was perched on the very top of her head.

"My God, Helen," I uttered in astonishment. "You look as though you have enlisted in the Albanian navy!!"

"Now don't you go making me laugh—" as she laughed in spite of herself.

"But why the uniform? You look so serious, are things going that badly?" We had put so much effort into these "Pushing for Desegregation" lunches that the previous encounters had been well received.

"I've got one of those feelings," Helen stated as she snuffed out one used up cigarette and lit another so swiftly that I didn't even have time to offer her a light. I had worked with Helen long enough to know that when she had one of those ESP warnings it nearly always turned out to be a harbinger of bad tidings.

Earlier as we had been discussing the speech with the Mayor, Helen had urged him to stretch out the "good for business theme" that had grown out of previous meetings. In the course of this discussion Helen came up with the phrase "too busy to hate." It would in time come to represent the Hartsfield saga in Atlanta, but the first time he used it at the hardliners' luncheon the phrase fell on deaf ears.

During the question and answer period it was quite obvious that a bunch of the cruder Segregationist stalwarts had conspired together to dominate this aspect of the session.

"Would you allow your daughter to marry a Negro, Mr. Mayor?"

"Sir, my daughter is married. It is my fervent hope that she would not commit bigamy with you or anyone else."

"Mayor; don't you realize that our Negroes here in Atlanta are happy and content? They will stay that way if the outside agitators would quit stirring them up."

"The white agitators coming into Atlanta are the problem. They want to use the city as a battleground to fight a losing cause— just as they did in 1864. As long as I am mayor of Atlanta nobody is going to destroy this town again. I will not allow Atlanta to fall into the hands of the rabble-rousers. I will not allow the destruction of any property owned by a citizen of Atlanta."

"Do you really believe, Mayor, that us good people are going to stand idly by and let you put Negroes in our white schools?"

"The Atlanta Board of Education is a separate political entity. The Board sets educational policy and levies its own taxes. It will be their decision to make on the Desegregation of city schools; however, if and when they are ordered to do so by the Federal courts I have every confidence the Board will comply and I will see to it that the Atlanta police assist the Board in their compliance. Or would you prefer to have bayonet-wielding U.S. Army troops running our schools?"

(This was a year before Little Rock's public schools were Desegregated forcibly with the use of Federal troops.)

All the questions directed at the Mayor were in this negative vein. Helen had suggested some more positive questions for members to ask and had been told by certain members they would do so, and then, these members had gotten cold feet and not even shown up. Also, a number of members had agreed to bring their wives to hear the Mayor, but none had done so.

When the question and answer session began there was little support for the Mayor and as the questions were posed lots of snide and vulgar comments were made in support of the questioner. The Mayor, seated at the head table, could not hear these obscene remarks and wouldn't have cared if he had, but Helen and I had no trouble in hearing them and Helen took some of the comments personally— she being the only woman in the room— and she felt some were directly aimed at her and I think she was quite right in that assumption; even so, the Mayor handled himself with such aplomb that at the end of the question and answer period he got a hearty round of applause for coming into the enemy camp to debate the issue, and I thought that was progress and the meeting taken in that context rather successful.

"That no good son-of-a-bitch!!! That no good son-of-a-bitch!!" On the sidewalk walking back to Helen's office— I had never seen her so enraged.

"He broke his word to me!! He broke his word to me! That no good—" I thought if Helen got any madder she was going to explode right there on the sidewalk.

Finally, she managed to quit cursing long enough to tell me what had happened. She had discussed the Mayor's appearance at the club with a member she knew well and had worked with before on an unrelated matter and he had said that wives would be invited and the questioning would not be left solely to the hardliners. Obviously, he could not pull this off so when he ran into resistance from the membership— he ran.

This happened all the time in Atlanta on the racial issue and I could not understand why Helen, of all people, could not accept that.

"You don't understand because you are a man. Men don't break their word to other men— and no man is going to break his word to me and get away with it. Mark *my words*: He will get his comeuppance."

Godfather had the inspiration for the meeting at the Piedmont Driving Club. He thought the coupon-clippers and old time Atlantans should get an up-to-date report from the Mayor on Desegregation. He let the word get out that he thought it important for people to attend the luncheon to hear the Mayor's report.

Around Atlanta, when Godfather let his wishes be known, things happened. We had a huge turnout.

Godfather did not appear. In Atlanta in the thirties and forties he was all over town and you could encounter him anyplace. By now, and by design, and because he had created so much wealth for Atlanta and for himself through Coca-Cola, everybody had to come to him. It was the mystique of the all powerful, the role of the Godfather.

"Why don't you try the banana pudding," I cajoled. Having failed to get Helen to eat any of the main course of the club's food, I was trying now to interest her in the dessert as I wolfed down a huge helping of what was a Helen favorite. But she would have none of it. While I had been ingesting as though World War III had reached the county line, Helen had been busily writing on a legal pad. When she finished she gave the paper to the waiter and told him to deliver it to the Mayor.

For his part, Hizzoner was having a blast, for he was seated at a table surrounded by a bevy of rich, pretty, Atlanta matrons who were ooooooooing and aaaaaaaahhhhhhhing over his every word—giving Helen another reason to be blue. I thought of kidding her about this but upon reflection decided it would be a bad move.

"You don't like this place because you are a political activist by birth. I'll bet if you had been born in the North you would have been a lawyer or a union organizer."

For the first time that day Helen's face lit up. "I would have been both!!! And damn good at it, to boot!!"

"So; that is the reason you don't like this place?"

"Now listen here, J.J., unlike you I'm not a historian and this place is a monument—a monument to the past. It has no heartbeat, no life, no soul. I have to be where life is pulsating."

"Like the Greyhound Bus Station?" Helen was famous for doing her shoe box polling at such places. She was also crazy about bus station food. The mustard was so tangy, she insisted.

The mayor's speech was a big hit that day with the ladies and gentlemen of the Piedmont Driving Club. As we left I happened to spot the yellow sheet of paper left on the table by the Mayor. It was the note Helen had written to him before he gave his speech. I retrieved this historical document in the hope that one day I could share its contents with generations then unborn. The note's message, less the salutation, repeated two-dozen times these three words:

> Dear William Berry—
> Duty! Honor! Country!

"Listen here, J.J., let's don't be in such a rush. I'm just famished. Could we stop by the Varsity on the way back to town for a couple of Chili dogs and a Coca-Cola?"

There is nothing more native to Atlanta than playing golf. Since Bobby Jones' heyday it had been the most popular form of recreation in the city, and with a mild Winter climate many enthusiasts played the yearround.

The city's public golf courses had always been reserved for whites. A group of black golfers wanted to play on city courses and had filed suit in Federal court to Desegregate them. Mayor Hartsfield met with African-American leaders and began planning a strategy that would open the courses to blacks by means of a well-worked out plan and in a peaceful manner.

Silly as it appears today, elaborate planning was necessary to bring about the peaceful Desegregation of the city's golf courses.

"I would plow up all those golf courses and plant them in peas" before he would see them Desegregated bellowed the Governor of Georgia. With sentiment such as this emanating from the highest political power in the state the difficult job of complying with the law of the land was made much more difficult.

The Mayor and the Chief had meetings with the white leadership of the city and black leaders. Closing down the golf courses was not an option, not in a city where people arose at dawn on weekends to beat the rush to the courses.

The black leadership of the city was agreeable to any plan that would Desegregate the golf courses without incident and agreed to make no move to integrate the courses until the city had an opportunity to work things out. It was up to the leadership of the city government to come up with a workable solution.

The Mayor and the Chief had many conferences with white Atlantans. There was no enthusiasm for Desegregation but there was agreement that outright defiance was foolhardy and would lead to violence.

That's not to say that there was not some white sentiment for closing down the golf courses, but the Mayor and the Chief managed to convince a thin majority that this was a negative approach. The Mayor argued that he wanted to move Atlanta forward not only in the field of race relations but in all areas, and you could not have progress in one without progress in the other. The Mayor was able to persuade people what was involved in this matter and to accept Desegregation. He managed, as a matter of fact, to sell Desegregation to white Atlantans as a package deal.

The Mayor hit on the idea of Desegregating the golf courses on Christmas Eve. He felt that this was a good time for action on an issue that was not what could be termed overwhelmingly popular. The fact that the Mayor came up (with Helen's input naturally) with such a suggestion is a pretty good indication of how much thought and discussion had gone into the resolution of this problem.

The Mayor and the Chief drove around the courses that afternoon, observing the situation. It was a fine day for golf and, as prearranged, several black foursomes played on each course crowded with white golfers, without incident. All the preparation paid off handsomely.

With each further black demand there was a growing stiffening of white sentiment. Next time it would not be quite as easy as it had been with the golf courses.

Without warning, a group of African-American ministers

boarded a bus in downtown Atlanta and sat in the "white only" section of the bus. The driver left his route immediately and drove the bus back to the transit garage, whereupon the ministers got off and departed.

There was a state Segregation law which stated that all seating arrangements on municipal conveyances were Segregated. State officials, not to mention the general public, were calling the Mayor and the Chief on the phone demanding that the Segregation law be enforced by Atlanta police.

The Mayor was right on top of the situation. He scheduled a meeting the following day with business leaders and transit company officials. Hartsfield wanted time to test the validity of the Segregation law in the Federal courts. To accomplish this he needed the cooperation of the black ministers.

The Chief phoned the leader of the group, the Reverend William Holmes Borders, and asked him if he would mind being arrested. He told the Chief that all of the ministers would agree to be arrested to end Segregation.

The Chief was in a tight spot and grateful for Borders' cooperation. The Governor had sent the Chief word ordering him to enforce the Segregation law on Atlanta buses and trolleys or else. Or else the Governor would order the Chief's arrest and send in the Georgia National Guard to enforce Segregation.

The only hope the city of Atlanta had to avoid bloodshed was the Federal courts. In order for the Segregation law to be challenged in the courts there had to be a test case— those in violation of the law had to be arrested. The Chief asked Borders and his group to come to the police station to have a test case made against them. Borders insisted that he send the Black Maria to pick them up. The Chief dispatched a white and a black officer to handle the situation. As the paddy wagon was leaving the station house the *Time-Life* representative in Atlanta clamored aboard. He wrote an article for *Life* about his ride in the first Integrated paddy wagon in the South.

In due course, while the law was before the courts no black Atlantan had attempted to Desegregate the buses, the Federal court held the Segregated seating law to be null and void. Then, the city's transportation system was Integrated peaceably. Everybody heaved a sigh of relief. The city had played for time and used the time granted them for constructive action.

But the state government now embarked upon a *massive resistance* policy. The state was spending vast sums of money and employing legal aid to defend every nuance of Segregation to the end. This stance on the part of state government riled the black community.

Spelman College, Morehouse College, Clark College, and Morris Brown College comprise the Atlanta University complex in the city of Atlanta. Students from these colleges decided to lead a protest march and confront the state government with a list of grievances at the state Capitol. The day chosen for the march was May 17, 1960, the sixth anniversary of the Supreme Court's 1954 decision outlawing Segregation in the public schools.

When word went out that the students planned to march, groups of irate whites came into the city from God knows where. Both groups were determined to make a stand to show their strength.

It required no genius to realize that Atlanta was a city teetering on the edge of violence. All efforts to have the students call off their march failed. Both the Mayor and the Chief pleaded with the Governor to meet with a delegation of the students to no avail.

The students left the university complex that afternoon in an orderly column of twos. Atlanta police were stationed all along the route and there was no trouble. The police had worked out in advance with the students the line of march as far as the Capitol. Everyone hoped that the students would change their minds and simply march through the city avoiding the Capitol entirely, for they were as aware as anyone else of the danger of the situation. The Governor and other state officials had issued statements literally daring the students to hold their protests on state property. Armed and angry whites had gathered on the Capitol grounds and state police had made no effort to dislodge them.

The Chief, standing alone, stationed himself in the middle of the intersection at the Amen Corner— an armed mob at his back, the students marching onward to the front.

When the lead column reached the Chief at the Amen Corner, he ordered them to turn left and march down Washington Street in front of the Capitol— and thus staying off state property and preventing a bloodbath.

Although the column had halted it had not turned. The noise was deafening, some of the students in the middle of the column were singing and those behind the leaders shouting to move onto the Capitol. The throng standing behind the Chief was chanting— daring the marchers to cross the line. The sound was like being at an outdoor rock concert.

Then, all at once, the column lurched forward for the Chief, after some heated discussion, had persuaded them to turn away from the Capitol and go down Washington Street and onto a rally at Reverend Borders' Wheat Street Baptist Church.

The students marched away and the mob stood there gaping in bewilderment—having been denied their fight. The forces of *massive resistance* had badly wanted violence to occur on the streets of Atlanta an event they felt sure would solidify white support against Desegregation.

Much had been at stake here: The safety and the lives of the college students, good race relations, and Atlanta's prestige before the nation and the world.

Almost eight years later to the day, the funeral procession for Martin Luther King, Junior, weaved its way along Washington Street in front of the Capitol, turning at the Amen Corner.

NINETEEN

AT LONG LAST FIRST-CLASS

It was late in the afternoon and we were seated in Helen's old wooden lawn chairs in the backyard of her home in mid-town.

Margaret Long, a columnist for the Atlanta *Journal* had stopped by to swap stories on what was going on in Atlanta. Helen's backyard in the Summertime was the gathering place for Atlantans dedicated to ending Segregation.

Margaret had begun her newspaper career in Macon, written a book touting Integration, and managed to get out of town barely before being burned out. She had become an activist by accident and had never really intended to be involved that much in the Movement. But as the only liberal columnist on the afternoon paper, Margaret had a tough row to hoe.

"I just know somebody is tapping my telephone," Margaret insisted. "I hear these crackling noises all the time. Sometimes it sounds like 'ka ka ka ka' and then it will go 'boop boop boop boop,' and then the other day, I swear, I heard somebody coughing—can you imagine? First of all having the gall to listen in on someone's private phone line, and then the bad manners to cough into one's conversation. I get so discouraged sometimes."

Helen and I managed to keep a straight face during Margaret's rendition of telephone tapping noises and looked sympathetic.

Now, this calls for a celebration," I heard Helen saying. "It is certainly not everyday that Margaret gets chosen for recognition by the FBI," and Helen was out of her chair and walking barefooted across the darkening lawn being very careful to maneuver around and avoid any lurking honey bees in the uncut clover.

While Helen was gone I told Margaret how much I had enjoyed her "onliest" column the week before, for she had written an entire column on the regional use of the word onliest. It was all presented in a very straightforward way, until, toward the end, she referred to the person who had been the major focus of the story as "the onliest Segregationist Republican on that side of the family." Admirers called Margaret the velvet harpoon. Her detractors called her much worse things.

Helen was back in the yard with a tray of Coca-Cola.

"Oh Lord," moaned Margaret. "I wish I had remembered to bring my flask."

"I wish you had too," I concurred. Helen was a teetotaler. Her idea of having drinks consisted of either warm Coca-Cola (she was always forgetting to re-fill the ice trays) or iced tea so weak you were never sure you weren't drinking slightly rusting tap water. On this occasion Helen was serving Coca-Cola in the glass with a single cube of ice.

"Very European," Margaret commented acidly as she sipped the tepid brew. "I go through hell all day at the paper for you and the damn Movement and come here to relax and this is what I'm offered for refreshment. It's a sin."

Being able to communicate with Helen out-of-doors was a Summertime bonus. You were spared being enveloped by cigarette smoke.

Smoking for Helen was a symbol of liberation and also for African-American women of the same era, who had to contend not only with oppression of women, but Segregation to boot.

Grace Towns Hamilton, Executive Director of the Atlanta Urban League, an African-American Atlantan who also counted distinguished white Georgians in her ancestry, had been actively in the business of working to end Segregation as long as Helen. They had been together since the time of the bi-racial church meetings at the Amen Corner. They were absolutely devoted to one another but a friendly rivalry existed between the two of them to see who could move Atlanta forward faster.

Helen always went about things in a professional, straightforward manner. Grace approached matters through "Southernness." It depended on the situation of whose way was best suited to deal with a particular Desegregation problem.

If Helen was certain her way was best she would complain to me that:

"Her Grace says we should do it this way," or "Her Grace is unhappy with this approach and wants to do it another way." I often found myself in the role of referee.

Problems arose because the two had decidedly different backgrounds. Being from North Georgia Helen tended to be a populist. Grace was a native Atlantan who was at the very top of the social summit of African-American Segregated life.

In many ways being an aristocrat herself, once the Segregation wall began to buckle, Grace could communicate with rich white Atlantans as well, if not better, than Helen.

Like in the matter of trying to get the Segregationist white members of the Atlanta Library Board to Integrate the Atlanta Public Library.

This battle was Grace's baby. But she had been unable to pull it off and had to call on Helen for assistance. Then, Helen took over and did the project her way. That was always Helen's method. It had to be her brier patch. On the matter of the library, Grace was miffed.

I found myself crammed in a small room of the public library with Dad, Helen, and Grace. The library board had met, discussed the matter of Integration as it had many times previously, and had failed once again to end Segregation in the Atlanta Public Library.

Dad had been in attendance to assure concerned members of the board that he could provide sufficient police personnel to guarantee everyone's safety should Desegregation occur.

And this was always the pattern. No Integration ever took place in Atlanta until Dad assured everyone that all out race war would not ensue.

The board had agreed to Desegregation with some limited restrictions. Grace had cut a deal with the white plutocrats on the board to accept these terms. She argued that once in the library without trouble these restrictions could then be negotiated out the window.

Helen would have none of this second-class nonsense. The board had to open the doors of the Atlanta Public Library to everyone. This, after all, was America. Even in Atlanta. This infuriated some of the board members.

Grace thought Helen's approach was endangering Desegregation, but Helen insisted the pro-Integration members of the board would eventually force the issue through if everybody stood firm.

This discussion, to me, seemed to go on for an eternity in this very tight, windowless room. With Dad, and Helen, and Grace lighting one cigarette after the other, people were going to think the building was on fire.

When asked my opinion I stated, blinking my eyes, and gasping for breath, that we had better vacate the premises before we all suffocated. They all stared at me silently for a few seconds and then continued their discussion.

As things turned out, Eliza Paschall had to come into the discussions and finally managed to negotiate the Integration of the Atlanta Public Library. But it was on similar terms that Grace had worked out earlier. Later, Helen had to go back and get rid of the restrictions.

"Why do I have to do everything twice?" Helen complained.

It is far easier to pinpoint what Hartsfield and other Atlanta leaders did than it is to figure out why they did it. They all had strong convictions that Segregation was not only bad for the South, but quite simply—wrong.

Simply put, Hartsfield did what he did and took the others along with him because he had the foresight that all his fellow Southerners of his generation lacked—to see clearly that to do otherwise would harm everybody in the South both white and black alike. Desegregation was obviously a good thing for blacks. Now we know that it was also a good thing for whites. When most white people saw it as a bad thing for whites, Hartsfield with vision into the future, saw just the opposite.

This is why he did what he did; he could see clearly when others could not. He was able to implement what he knew to be best for the people because of the extraordinary elements of his complex nature.

All of these innovators of change were relentless hard workers and most important of all probably, just a hell of a lot smarter than others in their fields. But they had to be, for like African-Americans and women, Southerners of their time had to try harder to succeed, and not only be capable but better than anyone else because they were operating from a historically regarded second-class place, and if they were not really the best then no one would take notice. The were all top professionals in their fields and operated in sharp contrast to the usual kind of Southern politician, cop, and businessman of their day.

When people from elsewhere identified the Southern policeman in their minds they saw Bull Connor of Birmingham, not Herbert Jenkins of Atlanta. Because Robert Woodruff never made speeches and shunned all forms of public recognition, outsiders were unaware that in stature Woodruff towered over all entrepreneurs in the South and nation. Southern public relations types were thought to be more with it, but few such people anywhere ennobled that profession as much as Helen Bullard. And those who thought that all Southern politicians were the buffoons of laughter and legend never encountered William B. Hartsfield, mayor of Atlanta. They had all come of age acutely aware that they were looked down upon by outsiders as inferior because they were Southerners. It was necessary for them to prove to themselves and everybody else that this was not so. Their natural allies became those who were looked down upon by everybody because they were black. They changed the face of Atlanta and overcame discrimination and the lingering belief by many that the South was a second-class place.

In the 21st century with the growing mobility of individuals all over the globe people of a different race, religion, and culture will be living within the borders of the same country. Many persons of diverse origin trying to live together on the same soil. They possibly will be able to do so peaceably because of what has transpired in Atlanta in the latter decades of the 20th century.

Three factors must be in place before a divided community in which a minority is oppressed by a majority composed of people who are of a different race, religion, or culture can become Integrated.

The first is economic. Significant change can occur only if supported by continuing economic growth. Atlanta leaders could never have orbited the city out of its pattern of the past had not the shiny green leaves on the magnolia trees in Hartsfield's downtown park not become, blinking, fluorescent, dollar signs.

Secondly, there has to have been in the past crossover behavior by some of the majority with the minority, for so long as people have a fortress-like mentality of US against THEM warfare between the two separate entities is inevitable.

In the South Native Americans, African-Americans, and European settlers although often socially separate have been economically and genetically joined since the beginning. Since members of each group had sex and produced offspring who were members of both groups it was not as easy in the South to categorize people. Southerners come in different shades of coloring, a more diverse ethnic make-up, and many are a part of the Native American, European, and African experience. Southerners mirror the world's population more than people living in any other part of the United States.

The third and final factor which must be in place for historically separate peoples to integrate is that both sides have leaders dedicated to ending separatism.

Without courageous leadership Atlanta would never have gotten off the launching pad. There always has to be a William Hartsfield, Anwar Sadat, or Nelson Mandela in a position of political leadership.

If in the present day we are sometimes daily reminded of how much farther we must travel it is sometimes helpful to stop and reflect for a moment upon how far down the road we have already journeyed.

TWENTY

THE DAWN OF DIVERSITY

Adversity at a very early age in life can provide the opportunity for the individual to follow a course otherwise not taken. It is the opportunity to be a part of a larger scenario; the means by which the ego and the I open like an umbrella and aim skyward.

Before I was old enough to enter grade school I contracted scarlet fever. Fifty years ago this dreaded childhood disease in its most virulent form was nearly always fatal because there was then no medical treatment to combat it. Usually the diagnosis did not even occur until the post-mortem, and although I was diagnosed as having the severest form of the fever there was nothing to be administered except cold compresses to the body and prayer for the soul.

When my case was reported to the authorities, the county health department rushed to our home in the West End and nailed a warning sign on the front door. No one seemed to know how I contracted scarlet fever because I had not been around anyone who had been exposed to the disease and nobody else in the family or in the neighborhood had scarlet fever either before or after I did.

I remember little but the terrible burning fever which became so intense that I felt I was passing from this life and entering a world surrounded by hovering angels. Actually the word had gone out at the Wednesday night prayer meeting at our church that I had died and several members of the choir had been in such a hurry to rush to the house that they had not taken the time to remove their choir robes and when they had gathered in the doorway to my room I imagined in my feverish state that I was having an out-of-body experience.

Although I survived the ravages of scarlet fever before the fever crested it became so intense that it blistered all the skin on my body which ultimately peeled away into great long strips and when I looked at myself in the mirror I appeared as though a runaway extra from the movie *The Night of the Living Dead.*

The medical opinion of the day on my case was bleak. Because I had suffered such a severe bout of the illness we were told that my heartbeat had been affected and my immune system weakened which would leave me susceptible to every disease which came my way—and this proved to be pretty much the case. However, to the surprise of almost everyone I recovered quickly from scarlet fever and was once again on the go.

Which led to a life profoundly different from that of my contemporaries because the near death experience ultimately moved me away from my generational orbit and hurled me farther and farther outward into the unknown.

All of us who worked to end Segregation regarded this battle as Phase One, and although we were totally united on that issue because of our divergent make-up our concept of life in Atlanta following the end of Segregation varied widely.

Mayor Hartsfield viewed the issue almost solely for the creation of a greater Atlanta. His most enduring and hardest-fought legacies—such as the Atlanta airport and the Buford Dam—were issues more important to Atlanta's future than during his own tenure at city hall.

In a speech to Atlanta business leaders in the fifties he painted a picture of a future Atlanta freed from the shackles of Segregation.

"All over this town, right here in this very spot where we are meeting today—tall buildings will rise, people will come from all over the country to work here, to live here and enjoy the good life Atlanta affords. And everybody will want to come here—conventions will be held in Atlanta—democrats and republicans will hold their conventions in Atlanta because we have so many good democrats and good republicans in Atlanta—In Atlanta we have room for everybody . . . and, all the sports teams will come to Atlanta—we will have a magnificent stadium and the World Series will be in Atlanta—and oh yes—Don't forget the Olympics—The Olympics will be held in Atlanta—Just think of it!!—The Olympics in Atlanta!!!—In the South!!! In the future all of this will be possible because Atlanta is leading the South and those who are determined to hold us back will be vanquished."

Hartsfield was the last great orator to be mayor of Atlanta, and although some outstanding public speakers have followed him in that office, none could match his level of persuasion. He was as good as FDR and better than anyone else. In the dim light of the past I can still hear that magnificent voice urging Atlantans onward. And then, shudder to think what Atlanta and the South would be like today without him as our leader in those days of crisis.

Not that it came about without cost. People say to me: "Wouldn't Mayor Hartsfield be amazed if he could see Atlanta today?" And I usually say: "Oh, he certainly would be amazed, all-right," and move on. But what would really amaze him is the way people dress, or more exactly, do not dress.

Mayor Hartsfield wore a suit and tie everyday. I doubt that during the years he was in office he even owned a short sleeve shirt. Everyday was a workday, even Sunday after church. At a Summer picnic in Grant Park with the thermometer hovering around 98 degrees he removed his coat and rolled up his sleeves but he did not loosen his tie—and he was the coolest person in attendance. Why did he do this? In order to survive. He was mayor 23½ years and everyday was a struggle to be re-elected. He could never let up for one moment and take the chance that in a second of inattention Atlanta would have her destiny taken away.

In the 1953 election for mayor of Atlanta, the opposition to the Hartsfield agenda flooded the city, and the state, and the region with little white cards which read:

My Wish For 1953
That I Was A Little Dog
And That Hartsfield was a Tree

Such a demanding schedule put such stress on the Hartsfield marriage that it virtually collapsed. It became impossible for Mrs. Hartsfield to compete with so demanding a mistress as the city of Atlanta.

For love and affection on a more mortal plain Hizzoner began a series of widely-known affairs with a number of prominent Atlanta women. Everyone was fearful that such behavior by the mayor in this era would damage Atlanta's reputation. But the press chose to ignore these relationships.

My theory concerning the stance of the press on Mayor Hartsfield's private life was a matter of the times. First of all, in the
fifties people believed that everyone had a right to privacy—politician or not. And secondly, the press felt Hartsfield's stand
against Segregation was the most important issue then facing
the nation and judged against that anything else just was of no
importance. I think this policy has always been true. If the people know that the political system is in crisis, and they believe a
leader can lead them out of that crisis—they just do not care
about anything else. But if the system is not in crisis and the
political leader is not all that popular—then the elected official's
private life becomes public even for no other reason than to fill
the void.

As the time when Atlanta's public schools would have to be
Desegregated drew nearer the tension heightened.

I had just come from the Paramount theater where a poor-
white country-boy named Elvis Presley that then not all that
many people had heard of, had been mobbed following his per-
formance when he walked unescorted from the theater.

I was re-counting this event to Mayor Hartsfield who was
keenly interested in anything going on in Atlanta. We were
standing out-of-doors in the parking lot of a downtown hotel
and were surrounded by a number of Atlantans. The mayor responded to my news with such anger that I was both dismayed
and surprised. He took the occasion to denounce rock and roll,
and, mounting several empty wooden Coca-Cola cases that were
nearby, took the time to tell a group of Atlantans what they
wanted to hear—that rock and roll was bad for Atlanta youth.
He received a tremendous roar of approval from the impromptu
audience. He was warmly received afterwards and there was
much handshaking all around. Before leaving, he grabbed me by
the arm as a way of thanking me for providing him the opportunity to say something to Atlantans that would garner their
hearty approval. The speech had nothing in the mayor's mind to
do with rock and roll. He could not have cared less. It was but
his way of thanking a group of white Atlantans for their support
in the battle to end Segregation. It was something he could give
to his constituency which required no great sacrifice on their
part.

It became the mayor's pattern. So long as they would give up
Segregation he would lead the way in opposing any other issue
Atlantans were against.

I mentioned to Helen that I was greatly concerned about the mayor's state of mind and hopeful he could hold on until school Desegregation was accomplished.

"Don't say that, and don't even *think* that," Helen admonished me. "You think *I* don't know? Why, I don't even hang up on him when he calls me at 7 am about something that could wait until later. And you don't think *I* don't know?

What I never really knew about Helen and the mayor was whether her anger over his affairs was more personal than her concern of its effect upon public policy. Nevertheless, the battle to change the Southern way of life ground forward.

We were at a funeral for one of the white women who had been a pioneer in the Movement. Afterwards, as I looked upon Helen Bullard, Dorothy Tilly, and Grace Hamilton, standing on the church steps and engaged in rapt conversation I wondered if history would record the enormous contribution of these most remarkable women and their efforts to make the world a better place to live. How do you tell someone about a person like Mrs. Tilly? A devout Methodist in the tradition of Warren Candler and Wideman Lee, she would stand up at church meetings and Bible study retreats and say things like: "Well now, we've talked about Jesus and we have prayed to God, now, we've got to talk about what we are going to do to end Segregation." This at a time when her fellow church members would not allow a black person to enter their home through the front door. Where did she find the strength and determination not only to say such things but work diligently to achieve her goals? President Truman was so impressed with Mrs. Tilly and her work that he appointed her in 1946 to the first committee ever on civil rights. Mrs. Tilly was one of two Southerners on the committee which issued its now landmark report: *To Achieve These Rights*.

Driving back to town from the funeral, I expressed my fears to Helen that history would ignore her work and that of others in the Movement.

After laughing uncontrollably for a spell Helen managed to reply.

"But J.J., that will be your function. Why do you think I keep you around?" And she kept on laughing. And then, "And when you write about us and you will—be kind!!" And she laughed even harder. This quote from Noel Coward made me laugh.

That night in the back yard Helen had to recount to Margaret Long our earlier conversation. When they could stop laughing

Maggie said: "Well, I have a better story than that. This woman comes up to me in the restroom at Rich's and says 'oh oh oh—it's so wonderful all you have done for all the colored people!!'—and I said to her: 'oh oh oh—I'm so glad you think so'!!" And the two of them were convulsed in laughter.

To the point: The leaders of the Movement were just in Phase One. They thought anyone was a dimwit not to realize that for so long as an entire race of men, women, and children were oppressed in the South no Southern woman of whatever color could ever be free. But this was Phase Two. The women were so better programmed than anyone then imagined.

I was with some friends at a black nightclub on Atlanta's Westside. We had gone there to hear another new singer whom even fewer white people then had ever heard of: Marvin Gaye.

The small club was packed to the rafters but we were enthralled with the music and experienced a kind of elation we had never felt before and whether this was due entirely to the music or from the black people smoking Pot (white Atlantans had not yet discovered what they would call Grass) would be difficult to say.

Upon exiting, we immediately realized that we were being followed by Periscope and two of his subordinates. Periscope was a detective in the Atlanta Police Department and so nicknamed by me because of his tendency to pop up most anywheres. For years, he made it his duty to follow me around hoping, I suppose, by intimidation to keep me from pushing to end Segregation.

My folks, determined to proceed with the orderly Desegregation of the city of Atlanta, continued their Sunday School teaching and speaking to other churches in an effort to gain as much support for the new policy as possible.

In this time my mother prayed a lot. Years later I asked her what she had prayed for the most.

"That Mayor Hartsfield would find a steady girlfriend."

Historians will think it presumptuous to find a parallel between the days of Pericles and the time of Hartsfield. No way that the Athens of Pericles and the Atlanta of Hartsfield could be similar. But we can at least hope that two millennia from now history will remember Hartsfield in much the same way as we today recall Pericles. Certainly all those who worked so long and hard to change things in the South would so believe.

In late August of 1961 the Atlanta public high schools opened

Integrated. Some half-dozen protestors were arrested for trying to disturb the process. The Media, in its finest show ever of civic responsibility, stayed away from the newly Integrated schools and classes began without incident. The forces of *massive resistance* although not defeated were severely crippled.

Around noon, Attorney General Robert Kennedy called Dad and thanked him on behalf of himself and the President and the nation. Later that day President Kennedy held his news conference and it was all over.

Even though our work was finished and I saw less of Helen and the others in the future, we did all come together once more. The occasion was the dinner honoring Dr. Martin Luther King, Jr., after he was awarded the Nobel Peace Prize.

When I entered the lobby of the hotel that night I walked right into the outstretched arms of Daddy King.

"Little Cap—How in the world are you?" And he gave me a real bear hug. "Oh, now, I musn't be calling you that anymore—" but just as quick he was rushing around telling everybody that Little Cap was present. Most of the early arrivals were the longtime business proprietors along Decatur Street that I had gotten to know years ago. It was like a neighborhood reunion.

As soon as I went upstairs I encountered Helen and the Superintendent of Detectives of the Atlanta Police Department. Both were ashen.

The hotel switchboard was flooded with bomb threat calls. The Atlanta police charged with protecting Dr. and Mrs. King were ordered to delay bringing the couple to the hotel until it was decided whether or not to evacuate the hotel and cancel the dinner.

Nobody knew what to do. When Dad arrived he ordered the hotel switchboard closed and for all the direct lines to be used for police business only. He then ordered that the dinner was to proceed on schedule but that Dr. and Mrs. King were to be brought to the hotel only after their route to, and entrance into the hotel, was completely secure.

The entire hotel area was blocked off. Many police officials and hotel personnel wanted the dinner cancelled. Dad, savvy to all the behind the scenes maneuvering by those who never wanted the honor to occur in the first place, said no twice more and ordered a particularly disgruntled employee out of the area.

Everyone assembled in the dining room continued to wait patiently, albeit somewhat nervously. Commotion at a side door caused people to look in that direction thinking the guests of honor had arrived; but no, it was *Journal-Constitution* columnist Celestine Sibley making a hurriedly late entrance.

By the time the King family arrived everything appeared normal but they were just being served dinner when Atlanta police stopped a car in the vicinity bearing an out-of-state license plate and upon searching the trunk had discovered enough dynamite to blow the hotel to smithereens. There was a worried conference in the kitchen amid the clattering of dishes and waiters rushing about. All the police on hand told Dad the building had to be evacuated because the driver of the dynamite-laden automobile had been positively identified as one of two brothers from Alabama who were members of a hate group and he had told police that the police had caught him but not the others. Once again, over vigorous protest, Dad ordered for the dinner to proceed. He called for more police to be stationed in the building and before the dinner ended practically all the police officers on duty were providing security.

When the Jewish rabbi, upon introducing the Catholic archbishop remarked that his Eminence arose from a sick bed to attend the dinner and the archbishop brushed this comment aside as nonsense, no one laughed harder than Dr. King—providing a moment of levity for a somber evening.

The oratory that evening was monumental. I thought Dr. Benjamin Mays, President of Morehouse College, in a brief address, captured the historical essence of the occasion better than others.

By the time the dinner was concluded Helen appeared as though she had aged 20 years because at her telephone station in the kitchen she had been privy to all the police calls. She often said afterwards that organizing and managing the King dinner had been one of the most grueling tasks of her life.

When I left the hotel that evening I encountered a young black woman standing on the sidewalk waiting to get a glimpse of the people coming out. Among other things, she said to me that "isn't it wonderful that while in the past we have been so backward tonight both black and white Atlantans were together for something like this." I told her that I heartily agreed.

POSTSCRIPTS

JANE

When the sewing room at Grady was eliminated and the hospital began purchasing ready-made uniforms and linens, Jane became house mother for the student nurses. At the age of eighty-eight when a protest movement she led at her retirement home failed to bring about improvement in the operation of the facility, she and three other residents in the dark of night went over the wall. She no longer cut her hair and in the last year of her life came to resemble more than ever her native American ancestors. I always thought she was preparing herself for whatever tough job assignment came her way in the Happy Hunting Ground.

ERNA

She outlasted the Segregationist years and managed to help maintain the Health Department's record as the most progressive in state government. She inherited the Mason homeplace in the Indian Fields and lived to see a great-grandson of Ellery's and Almanza's, Wayne Mason, as Chairman of the Gwinnett County Commission in the 1970s, bring running water made possible by the Buford Dam throughout the county—whose red clay fields had been abandoned to scrub pine—to become in the 1980s, the fastest growing county in the United States. In the mid-nineties the population of Gwinnett County exceeded that of the city of Atlanta.

GODFATHER

When a lady asked Miss Nell, Robert Woodruff's wife of forty years, if she regretted not having any children, she told the woman she was mistaken: That the Woodruffs had a very large family for they regarded as their family all of the children of Atlanta.

MAYOR

Upon retiring as mayor following the successful Desegregation of Atlanta's schools, Hartsfield travelled the globe tirelessly promoting Atlanta. In his seventies and a grandfather, he married a widow with a young son. When the first Willie B. died Zoo Atlanta acquired another gorilla naming him also Willie B. For twenty-five years Willie B. had to live alone before Zoo Atlanta provided him with a female companion. In 1994 Willie B. became a father for the first time. Hizzoner would have been very proud.

CHIEF

Following the riots over civil rights in the 1960s, Herbert Jenkins served as the only police officer on the Kerner Commission, appointed by President Lyndon Johnson, the commission found that America was two separate societies: One white and one black. He was a senior research associate at Emory University for a decade. Three years after the death of Margie, at the age of 82, he died from a self-inflicted gunshot wound.

CHIEF JENKINS GAVE CITY A GREAT GIFT—ITS REPUTATION

Over the last quarter of a century, writers, scholars and political leaders have sought to explain the distinctive qualities that have made it possible for Atlanta to escape the violence and bitterness that wracked so many other cities during the civil rights confrontations of the 1960s.

Obviously, no single answer suffices; but a sensitive observer could have found most of those distinctives embodied in one man.

Herbert T. Jenkins Sr. was Atlanta's police chief from 1947 until 1972; and, as such was in a key position to exert leadership—for good or bad—in an era charged with anger, a time when a single misstep could set off a conflagration.

As a white police chief he was the most visible symbol of the power that had kept blacks in subjugation for centuries. The strategy of confrontation adopted by Martin Luther King Jr. and other civil rights leaders made him a natural target.

But Herbert Jenkins believed that the first duty of a police officer was not to preserve Segregation, but to keep the peace, to protect all the citizens of his city from violence.

He demanded respect for the law. In doing so, he was largely responsible for giving the city the gift that made its future prosperity possible—a reputation for tolerance and racial harmony that has become its greatest asset.

Excerpted from the Atlanta *Journal*
From the column of Durwood McAlister
July 24, 1990

MARGIE

Always interested in family history, she spent her retirement years doing genealogical research. When Alex Haley galvanized the country to study its generations past, she assisted others in their quest. Women in sensible shoes and flip-up sun glasses laden down with tote bags—their shoulders bent from the weight of the burden of having to tote their ancestors around— were always turning up at her doorstep. I encounter people and they say: "Oh, I knew your mother. She helped me find my roots."

GRACE

Grace Towns Hamilton was the first African-American woman to be elected to the Georgia legislature. She served with great distinction for many years.

HELEN

The year the Atlanta schools were integrated, Helen's political coalition elected Ivan Allen mayor. Allen, mayor of Atlanta during the tumultuous 1960s, was the catalyst that launched Atlanta into becoming an international city. When Stone Mountain was designated as a state park Helen pleaded, without success, to have the memorial carving honoring Confederate leaders also include Grant and Sherman thus transforming the old rock so long associated with the Klan, into a national memorial—like Arlington. Helen's greatest legacy to Atlanta was in persuading political leaders to spend the first available educational funds of the 1960s on creating something that the community did not have, and which, over the years, would grow into a colossal scientific educational facility—the place all Atlantans know and cherish as Fernbank. Without Helen's steely determination the project would never have blossomed. Nearly twenty years after Helen's death, former 1950s Governor and United States Senator Herman Talmadge, the son of Eugene Talmadge, who also served as governor of Georgia, the two most outspoken advocates for Segregation in the South, was quoted in the Atlanta *Journal*: "When slavery was abolished, if we had made first-class citizens out of blacks at the time, it would have been much better." Somewhere in the not forgotten soul of the universe I could hear Helen repeating her favorite prayer: "Better to have at long last seen the light than to die blind."

MARGARET (MAGGIE) LONG

Once the battle to end Segregation was over white Southerners had to adjust to the fundamental change in Southern life. For the small army of white Southerners whose lives had been dominated by the struggle a different kind of adjustment was necessary because victory over Segregation meant demobilization. We were like soldiers who had been discharged and sent home now that the war had ended. As in all such instances, some veterans made the transition to civilian life more easily than others. No one had a harder time adjusting than Margaret Long. She no longer wrote a column for the paper because as she herself stated she no longer had anything important to write about. For someone who had engaged the enemy on the field of battle and dodged bullets from the age of nineteen, and not only survived but lived to write about it, victory was ruinous. Although she tried mightily to engage a newer foe, none save the enemies from within ever really engaged her. When she died no honor guard saluted, no bugler blew a last farewell for this brave soldier who fought long and hard so that others might live free. All the women in this book who worked to end Segregation are but a microcosm of the women of the South of the time. It was the Southern woman who was the crucial and deciding factor which changed the Southern way of living. We know this because of what happened in Atlanta in the 1960s was the exact opposite of what happened in Atlanta in the 1860s. Had the women of Atlanta been as uninvolved and submissive on the subject of race in the 1960s as they had been in the past, the outcome of the Second Battle of Atlanta would have been quite different. All of us who live in Atlanta and the South today are forever in their debt.

CHARLES BELL

Charles Bell was one of the first Americans to join the Peace Corps. He was living and working in South America with his wife and young daughter when President Kennedy was assassinated. He died two days later of a heart attack. Charles Bell was twenty-eight.

Index